Praise for *Finding Right Work*

Leni Miller has written a gem. She shows us how to silence the inner fears and find our own voice—and demonstrates how to enjoy the process. The book is at once practical and a wonderfully enjoyable read, a rare combination for a work that provides such a profound result. Read this book every morning until you wake up delighted with what you do in the world.

> — **Terry Pearce**, founder of Leadership Communication and author of *Leading Out Loud: A Guide for Engaging Others in Creating the Future*

Finding Right Work is brilliant. It will guide you through discovering and building a great life and your right work. I find myself returning to it over and over whenever I need some wisdom to help me on my journey.

> — **Louann Brizendine** MD, founder and director UCSF Women's Mood and Hormone Clinic and author of the best-selling books *The Female Brain* and *The Male Brain*

Right Work is the secret to lasting happiness—and in *Finding Right Work* Leni Miller tells us how to find it! I have been blessed to be in my right work most of my life and that has truly made all the difference. I highly recommend that you read this masterful and inspiring guide ASAP and keep it close for years to come.

> — **Chip Conley**, founder of Joie de Vivre, speaker, and author of *Peak: How Great Companies Get Their Mojo from Maslow* and *Emotional Equations: Simple Truths for Creating Happiness*

In *Finding Right Work*, Leni Miller strikes just the right balance between inspiration and perspiration. Readers will be both entertained and set in motion.

> — **Larry Stupski**, former chief operating officer, Charles Schwab and Company

Finding Right Work is a lovingly woven tapestry of inspirational stories, practical steps and pragmatic advice that is like a magical gift from your fairy godmother. Follow Leni's wise advice carefully and chances are you will live happily ever after.

> — **Bonny Meyer**, co-founder of Silver Oak Cellars, owner of Bonny's Vineyard, philanthropist

Are you living a life that is not quite whole, not totally fulfilling? *Finding Right Work* will be your lifeline, helping you create a life you love!

> — **Dickson C. Buxton**, founder of Private Capital Corporation and author of *You've Built a Successful Business, Now What?* and *Lessons in Leadership and Life—Secrets of Eleven Wise Men*

Leni Miller lives by her value of doing right work and finding joy, freedom, and ease in doing so. In this inspiring and practical book, she acts on her mission of helping others find their right work, whatever their age and experience. I highly recommend *Finding Right Work*. Read it and you'll learn practical steps to moving past the fear and inertia that keep too many people chained to jobs that drain them emotionally, physically, and spiritually.

> — **Mary Huss**, publisher, *San Francisco Business Times*

FINDING RIGHT WORK

FINDING RIGHT WORK

FIVE STEPS TO A LIFE YOU LOVE

Leni Miller

Foreword by John Racanelli

ISBN 13: 978-0-615705-95-8
ISBN 10: 0-615-70595-2

Cover design by Susan and Chloe Pate, Pate International
Interior design by Helen Glenn Court, Formandsubstance.com

Dedicated
to
my family
with special thanks
to
my grandmothers
Edith Walton Herrick and Helene Dieterich Woske
my father
Harry Max Woske
and
my daughter
Abigail Miller Tollefson

CONTENTS

FOREWORD

Most of us rationalize our work despair with the old saw that "if it were fun, it wouldn't be called work." Encumbered by mortgages, tuitions, and plain old fear, we write off this drudgery as the cost of doing business. Then, of course, if we're out of work completely, we "need to find a job."

With vague apprehension and a twinge of regret, we settle for this disquieting and—for many of us—chronically dysfunctional relationship to our work life. All too often, that infects the rest of our life as well: our physical and mental health, our capacity to love, and our ability to enjoy the limited time given to us.

Even our success conspires against us. We're led to believe that if we really pursue the deep yearning we have for more meaningful work, or if we pass up the job being offered to us, we might lose what we have right now. We shudder at the thought of giving up these little baubles of pleasure. Believe me, I know. I was there not so very long ago.

Then I met Leni Miller. Over the course of several conversations, she opened my eyes to the concept of Right Work, patiently leading me through the five steps described in this book. Quite frankly, my life will never be the same. It has changed in a radical and incredibly positive way.

I agreed to write the foreword to this book because I've often wished other people could reap the benefits that Leni's extraordinary insights gave me, insights based on her forty-year career helping people find their right work. As surely as you hold this book right now, I hope you will someday look back on the moment you found Leni Miller, as I did, and know that you found a gem. All you have to do is look.

It was a long road to finding my own right work. I grew up in northern California with an early and lifelong passion for the ocean. My love of the sea runs deep. I have been a surfer and scuba diver since my teenage years. I'm an avid open-water swimmer and have made the infamous Alcatraz crossing twelve times. I've also been an ocean sailor, navigator for a 6,000-mile voyage aboard a tall ship, professional diver and king crab fisherman in Alaska's forbidding Bering Sea. I've led adventure travel expeditions to Peru's Machu Picchu, Canada's San Juan Islands, and the Caribbean. It's no secret to those who know me that love of the ocean runs in my veins.

In recent years, I've keenly felt the pain of seeing firsthand the dramatic degradation of that life-giving ocean. Our human impact on the world's aquatic treasures has viscerally affected me, to the core of my being. Over time, I tried to give voice to this as best I could, volunteering my time and talent for conservation organizations focused on the ocean and San Francisco Bay. Important though they were, I knew all my efforts were a mere drop in the bucket. I was only barely serving my life's greatest passion, and I knew it.

Enter Leni Miller. She taught me how to apply the steps she outlines in her book, *Finding Right Work: Five Steps to a Life You Love*. She helped me with powerful exercises in self-discovery, unlocking the key to who I really am in terms of my work. And she helped me develop a plan to identify and actually find that work, providing a course in self-discipline and understanding that gave me the courage and determination to see it through to completion. She and the content of this extraordinary book helped me make it happen.

Today, as CEO of the National Aquarium, I live and work in service of the ocean I've always loved. I get to spend my days working with a community of progressive people who share an intense and deep commitment to our blue planet's life support system. I love my work and am able to leverage my passion, experience and skills in ways I might never have dreamt possible before I met Leni. Thanks to the course she put me through—that of finding right work—my strongest talents and values are reflected in the work I now do. In fact, I often catch myself thinking, "Do I really get paid to do this?"

For me, it all came down to letting go of the need to know exactly what my work would be and how I was going to find it. Once I learned to be crystal clear about my gifts, priorities, talents and values, the work I was meant to do actually found me! I can tell you: the steps outlined in this book are easy to understand and pay off quickly. They work. If you commit to the process described in *Finding Right Work*, stay on-point, and have faith in the outcome, you can find your own right work and live the life you love.

Leni has recorded her lifetime of wisdom, along with dozens of stories about real people like you and me, that will take your understanding of what is your right work to a more psychologically and spiritually sophisticated level. Perhaps more importantly, it can turn the dreaded concept of work into a joyous part of your life. The process and stories Leni tells here are a gift—one that I can truly say has changed my life for the better. I am thankful for the wonderful changes her message has made in my life, and I believe you will be, too.

—John Racanelli
  September 2012
  Baltimore, Maryland

PREFACE

*Don't ask what the world needs. Ask what makes you come alive,
and then go do that. Because what the world needs is people who
have come alive.*

HOWARD THURMAN, AMERICAN AUTHOR AND PHILOSOPHER

Do you want a fresh start? Are you longing for work that makes your heart sing? Are you trying to find exactly how you fit in the work world? You are not alone. In my business, I see a continuous stream of people who are (consciously or not) searching for their right work, work that they can love, work that will sustain and satisfy them, and in which they can give their greatest contribution. For some people, only a little nudge is needed to steer them in their right direction; others need encouragement and an impetus to carve out the time and energy required for soul searching and long-term planning. The difference between these two extremes often has less to do with the actual work being sought than with the individual's personality, mindset, timing, and attitude. Certainly some jobs are less abundant and some work is more difficult to start than others, but my experience has taught me that a person's right job or right work is always out there—somewhere.

I have been in the job placement and search business since 1973, working with prospective candidates searching for the next right job and clients in need of the right employees. In every field and every time, candidates and clients alike were seeking the right match in the workplace. I have interviewed thousands of job candidates over the years. I've interviewed people who had been dragging themselves to jobs they hated, some of whom secretly didn't believe it was possible to be happy and have a job at the same time. Whenever I was able to place them in jobs they loved, jobs that energized them and made use of their talents, it was an absolute joy to see their transformation. Those positive changes rewarded me and kept my interest in job placement and the workplace strong. I believe in the importance of right work so strongly that when it seemed the media had nothing but bad news about the job market, I countered this negativity by co-producing a television series called "Home Sweet Office," highlighting the inspiring stories of people who made dramatic and innovative shifts in their ways of working by leveraging technology and their own creativity to create lives they loved. I fully understand what a joy right work can be.

All too often, people stay in work they hate, work that doesn't challenge them, work in which they are not using their talents, simply because they don't know the steps they need to take to find something better. I've found that whether one is looking only for income or is looking for right work—work that best uses one's gifts, skills, and talents and that aligns with personal values and priorities—finding and creating that work requires a handful of careful steps. For some people, these are steps into completely new territory. For everyone, these are steps to practice multiple times and execute over time. Why the practice? Our minds are filled with old habits of thinking, ways of viewing how the world and our lives are. Yet change is constant and those habits of our minds can quickly become outdated. As we mature over time, our life priorities shift, what we're searching for changes, and the nature and demands of work itself evolve. Our minds sometimes don't keep up with changes in our lives, in the world, or in the job market— and yet those changes are there, all the time.

As specific jobs and even the concept of a long-standing job are disappearing, new ways of working are evolving. Consultants and contractors are creating opportunities by offering new services and weaving unique fabrics of services together. I have plenty of firsthand experience in this trend, for I have re-imagined and transfigured my own career to adapt to the widespread use of new technology and of economic cycles over the years and, more recently, to accommodate my own changing priorities and interests. I have helped generations of people re-invent their careers and create their own right work. I've learned that a big secret is to become comfortable with change, for it's unavoidable; in fact, it's imperative for life and for happiness. Just think how dramatically job descriptions and the job market have altered over the years—more rapidly now than ever before. Change and flexibility are key—and the truth is, that's always been the case.

For more than four decades, I have helped job seekers on their way to right work. I can tell you that while the steps may appear simple, they take practice, reflection, and a new relationship with your own mind. I can predict that, just as a toddler taking those first steps, you may feel a little wobbly in the process of changing, learning, and growing. I can also predict that as you keep practicing, you will soon find yourself falling fewer times, then walking more purposefully and confidently, and ultimately living your way into work that is right for you.

In *Finding Right Work: Five Steps to a Life You Love* you'll find a guide to the process of finding right work, illustrated by real stories of those who have successfully walked these steps and created work and lives they love. You'll find yourself in good company as you read of those who have methodically moved through the steps and those who have simply leapt, scrambled in mid-air, and landed on the steps en route to their right work. You'll read of people of all ages who have changed their lives for the better as they changed their work. You'll read of people who changed their work by changing their attitudes. You'll read of people I've known and people I've coached as they took incremental steps to discovering right work, as they juggled their day jobs while using weekends and nights to know and grow their dreams, as they found balance and satisfaction.

As you'll see, you are not the first person (nor is yours the first generation) to give yourself permission to step out into right work. Why wait? Why confine yourself by looking only for a "regular" job when you can find a job or create your own work that fits you perfectly? You can decide to customize your own work life in a way that could be more lucrative and liberating than any previous work experience or job could have been.

Having personally experienced, professionally coached, and written about many remarkable career changes, I thought I was adept at predicting how people were likely to have made the changes that got them to their own right work. But sometimes life throws surprises. This particular surprise was a friend and a neighbor. Jim Woessner and I had lived across from each other for years. I knew he had been a nuclear engineer for Pacific Gas & Electric and that he now traveled to Oregon on contract engineering assignments for at least one week a month; I also knew that he led creativity workshops in his floating home's art studio, and that he was a gifted painter, poet, and sculptor. But it wasn't until he told me of a watershed moment in his life that I had any sense of the dramatic actions he had taken to get where he is today.

When he was employed by PG&E, Jim and his wife often went away on weekends so that Jim could decompress from the stress of his job. After one weekend, as he was driving home to the San Francisco Bay Area, Jim realized that his stomach felt progressively worse with each mile. At age forty, he had been struggling with health issues for some time, and it suddenly hit him that something had to change drastically—and soon.

That next week Jim headed out to lunch, as he had every day, but this day, he never returned to his office. Years later, when he told me the story, I was shocked, and asked incredulously, "You just didn't go back?"

"That's right," Jim answered. "I didn't know I wasn't going back. I didn't plan it. I just walked out the door. It wasn't until I got to the corner of Market and Beale Streets in San Francisco that I realized I had my briefcase with me. It was filled with probably ten pounds of memos, meeting minutes, various reports, and proposals. It was typical of the weight that I would carry with me every time I left the office. I looked down at the briefcase in my hand, and saw that I was still literally attached to everything all those years in corporate America represented. I knew that I had to get rid of the briefcase. I'm not proud of what I did in terms of the environment, but in the moment, it was the most magnificent of feelings. I whirled the briefcase out of my hands and watched as it spun away like a discus. I remember seeing it arc up in what seemed like slow motion over Beale Street, over rushing traffic, over parked cars on the other side. I remember seeing it hit the ground and slide on the pebble-textured sidewalk. Those pebbles acted more like ball bearings than little pieces of gravel and they just kept the briefcase moving. It slid on and on, all the way to the waterfall at 77 Beale Street, the home of Pacific Gas & Electric. The second that the briefcase hit the stone base of the corporate waterfall, its lid sprang open and all those papers of mine got caught in an updraft. I watched the paper fly up and up and up, dispersing in every direction imaginable. I just stood there watching. To me, it seemed like they were doves, white doves, flying out of my battered old briefcase. And then I heard a honking horn, turned, and saw my wife drive up. I got in the car, and never went back."

I had heard many end-of-work stories over the years: this one topped them all and left me speechless. After a pause, Jim quietly added, "And I can tell you something else. This happened at precisely 1 PM, February 8, 1991."

I sat in awe of the power and courage of Jim's actions. In my mind's eye, I could see those papers circling heavenward. I could sense the relief and release that Jim had felt upon seeing those papers fly up, symbolically freeing him from a kind of prison in which he had lived for so many years.

Jim told me that he had no idea what work he would do next. He hadn't planned to leave. He hadn't planned a next step. He knew only what he never wanted to do again. And he left that behind. He had jumped off a very big cliff and managed to do it without an ounce of fear. The pain of Jim's present had become bigger than any fear of his unknown future. It was so big that it had begun to make him sick. Later, I pictured the scene as a parallel to the opening scene of the classic Mary Tyler Moore television show, in which Mary strides briskly through Minneapolis before smiling, spinning, and tossing her hat up in the air while the theme song in the background affirms, "You're gonna make it after all!" Unlike Mary, Jim was permanently leaving his job, but from my perspective years later, his moment of launching that briefcase seemed to pack the same exuberance and optimism as Mary's moment and theme song. I knew that Jim had made it and was quite successfully melding his apparently disparate gifts—nuclear engineering expertise, artistic skills, patience, and his unique point of view—in his life.

Memorable as Jim's departure from the corporate world of PG&E was, I'm not recommending that you allow yourself to reach a parallel point of desperation; in fact, reading this book should keep you from just that. Along the way, you'll read of people whose paths to right work were markedly different than Jim's. You'll see that for all of them—young, older, and in-between—the change and the long-term happiness and freedom are very real. Be assured that while the steps described in this book are considerably less dramatic than hurling your briefcase across a city street, they are every bit as liberating—and they provide a direct and considerably less disruptive path to your right work.

Are you just starting out and looking for that first job, venturing into your first career? Are you reentering the workforce? Are you newly retired from a long career and ready for a new phase? Are you unsatisfied with the direction of your current career and wondering how best to identify what you really want to do next? Are you feeling as though the work world as you've known it is fast disappearing? Are you a new college graduate, about to enter the workforce? Are you fresh out of the military and looking for what's next? Are you dissatisfied with your current job or sense a downsizing on the horizon? Are you dreaming of an entirely new challenge, one that's more in line with your strongest talents or your changing priorities? Are you worried that you can't have work you love and pay the bills? Are you ready to discover your own right work or the job of your dreams? Are you ready to finally set your own path and create a life that you positively love? If yes, read on!

No matter where you are now, how old you are, how inexperienced, how experienced, how optimistic, or how discouraged, the advice and guidance in *Finding Right Work* can change your life. As you read the chapters and work through the Action Items, you will be charting a course to your right work. Whether you're planning a slow transition or are in need of right work right now, you can use the same five steps that have led many people before you to their own right work, work that they love. The five chapters of *Finding Right Work* describe those steps, one to a chapter, each with stories of real people as they mastered the step and whose experience highlights the step. The epilogue provides further information on putting the five steps into action and making them work for you.

Simple as these steps may seem as you read them, they can be surprisingly challenging. Using them requires uncovering and changing very old habits of the mind, identifying fears, and embracing change with courage and conviction. In coaching people through the process, I've learned that people are more successful with the five steps if they have small, specific Action Items to work through as they're learning to travel the five steps to their right work. For that reason, the second section of the book delineates detailed Action Items for you to undertake on your journey of identifying and finding (or creating) your own right work. Brief sneak peeks into the Action Items follow each of the first four chapters.

How you use this book is up to you. You may derive the most from it by reading the chapters straight through as an overview, before turning to the Action Items; then, as you work on the Action Items, you may want to revisit relevant steps. Or you may find that you've already moved through a step or two or that you'd prefer to tackle the steps in a different order than presented here. There's nothing magical about the order, per se; it's the accumulated effect of the steps and the Action Items that bring results. As with taking physical steps, you first have to want to move forward, have to give yourself permission, and have to begin. That permission to begin discovering your right work is key. Permission—constant, renewing permission—is what will keep you going throughout your journey. That permission is critical to what ultimately guides you to be who you really are and to your own right work. Slow or fast, now is the time to take the steps in *Finding Right Work* for yourself. By committing to the practice of the Action Items, you will strengthen your courage and conviction. Once you understand the process ahead, the possibility of finding or creating right work will become more real. Once the possibility of right work becomes more real to you, magic will begin to happen. You will be helped by many seen and unseen supporters; with their help, you will hear your own answers, answers that will help you be in touch with who you really are and what talents and gifts you can and want to give to the world.

Introducing people to these steps in person and helping them on their way is my passion and my right work. And, for many years, my internal voice has been supplemented by a chorus of friends and clients telling me to write about these steps to right work. My hope is that, through this book, I will do my part to ensure that the number of people living their right work grows exponentially. My dream is that the refrain I hear from people in their right work—"I just love what I do. I can't believe I get paid for this!"—will become your refrain. My intention is that you will feel, as I do and as so many of the people I've interviewed and worked with do, that you are blessed to be able to use your gifts and your energies in service to the world and yourselves; that you have the money you need and want; and that your heart sings much of the time.

By picking up this book, you've already begun the journey toward living more fully, finding connection, finding purpose, and finding your own right work. Now, I urge you to read *Finding Right Work* and commit to the process. Give yourself complete permission to embark on the adventure of discovering your talents and the full depth of what you are called to do in this world. You will never regret the decision!

—Leni Miller
September 2012
Sausalito, California

Leap and the net will appear.

JOHN BURROUGHS, AMERICAN NATURALIST

You take one last look up, and then quickly look down at the ground. You feel prepared. You have the skills to do this. You've watched others do it and know in your mind that you too can do it. Even so, you are frightened. This is something you have never done before. You grab the sides of the ladder and climb slowly and purposefully higher and higher. Your eyes remain down, staring at the rungs as you slowly climb, one foot at a time, two feet on each rung, one after the other. Finally, you reach the top of the ladder and step onto the long narrow board. With shoulders back and deep breaths belying what is feeling like abject terror, you reach the end of the precipice. You look down over the edge.

It seems like long moments pass. People are coming behind you. It's your turn. You take one last deep breath and then . . . you push yourself off the board, hold your nose, and take your very first jump into the deep end of the pool from the high dive. Remember the moment?

I remember it well. My fear had been there with me and we jumped together anyway. And I remember being so proud of myself. I remember too that the second and third and fourth jumps became easier and easier. Not long after that first jump, I jumped with joy. Years later, when my little sister climbed the ladder for the first time, I said to her, "Shirley, don't worry. It gets easier each time you do it and then it is really fun!"

The fact is, each of us has already jumped off of many high dives or cliffs in our lives.

When we first left home and started kindergarten, we jumped off of a cliff. Sure, we may have been told what we'd do there, may have even visited the school, but we didn't really know. We didn't know how we'd feel, what it would really be like, or if we'd like it. When we moved on to first grade, we jumped off another cliff. When we stood in front of the class or an audience in a school play for the first time, we jumped off a cliff. When we graduated from each grade and stage and moved forward into the next, we jumped off a cliff. When we left home and ventured out into the world, to college, or our first job, we jumped off a cliff. If we got fired or downsized, we got shoved off a cliff. When we retire, we jump or get pushed off a cliff. The cliffs are everywhere; they're part of life.

Making the decision to jump and overcoming that initial fear are often the hardest parts. The release and the joy that come with having made the leap, having successfully made it over the precipice: that's the positive memory to hold on to.

Over my years of interviewing, I have spoken with many people who have stayed in the wrong job because they simply could not overcome their fear of jumping. Many of them believed that there was no point, no upside, to leaving a miserable but "secure" job for the perceived black hole of the unknown. I have also interviewed and known many people who have become veteran jumpers and have readily leapt off of many different career cliffs. Guess who is happier?

Are the people stuck in jobs they hate or those unable to find their right work any different in intelligence, skills, experience, or background than those who love their lives and have found right work? No! Then what is the difference? The biggest difference is simply this: those who have found work they love have faced their fear of change, fear of the unknown, and started the journey. They have been willing to jump off of ledges or cliffs of old ways of thinking, working, and living . . . into the space of the unknown. They have climbed those stairs, taken that deep breath, and jumped. Many weren't certain which pool they'd land in; some didn't have a clue. But they all had faith in the process, believed they'd survive, and chose to think that where they landed would be better than what they were leaving behind. For them, the fear of the future had become less than the pain of the present.

You have already started. By standing at the bookshelf or ordering online, opening this book, and now reading—perhaps taking a few big breaths along the way—you have decided to climb the ladder and are taking a big step towards your next jump, the leap from your past into your future. Congratulations! You have taken the first and most important step: you have given yourself permission to find your right job, and to create your right work. You have jumped.

I promise that, as I've heard said so many times over the years, "When you jump off the cliff, the earth will rise to meet you or . . . you will learn to fly!" I'm here with you and I have over forty years of experience helping people understand what is or isn't their right work. I know the steps you can take that will lead you to your right work. Come with me and read real life stories of others who have jumped and found work they love: work that uses their unique talents, supports their life priorities, their financial needs, and reflects their values. Each of these people overcame many fears and challenges. Each of these people took the necessary steps to discover what was their right work. It is my hope that by reading their stories and with this book as your guide (think of it as a virtual coach), you'll be inspired to learn and use the steps, understand how to navigate them yourself, and discover the joy of work that is right for you.

Back to that diving board: chances are, the first time you had to be coaxed or encouraged into leaping off of it. And you probably had seen someone do it before you, bigger kids who were jumping with joy. Maybe you had even seen someone else take her first jump and bob up smiling. You knew you could swim well enough, but what about the jump and the time underwater? That was new. You (or a trusted friend) had checked out the conditions, made sure the environment was right. You might have even gone through a mental checklist—was the water deep enough, warm enough, suit on tightly enough—until there were no more questions or excuses. And then the leap.

With that first leap, whether you were jumping off a high dive or jumping off a rock ledge, chances are good that you had someone looking out for you, showing you how to make sure the jump itself was safe and you had the skills. But what if you don't have that prep time for examining the water depth, looking for hidden rocks, checking the steps, the board, the ledge, the height in advance? Or the skills to be confident that you'll be OK after the leap? Or even the assurance from friends and bystanders that it will be fun? And yet in all but the most dire circumstances, even if you slip off the high dive, chances are you'll land safely. Embarrassed, maybe, but safe (assuming you know how to swim).

But what if you slip off a career cliff or get kicked off? By yourself, by others, or because of some cosmic combination? Consider the story of a young woman who had struggled through her first year of nursing school and then begun her second. In contrast to some of her classmates, it wasn't the coursework that was difficult for Liz, or the school's culture; she was well prepared for both. The academics were not a problem, she was a natural helper, she had successfully volunteered in hospitals for years, she felt she knew what was ahead and was prepared. But, much to her surprise, the vastness of the suffering she saw in her training threatened to completely overwhelm her. Her personality was not just empathetic, it was empathic: she easily felt the pain and suffering of others as her own.

She was getting through nursing school on sheer willpower, partly due to her fear of disappointing her father and partly because the other five career paths readily available to women in 1968 didn't appeal to her either. Outside of nursing, what was there for her? She didn't want to be a social worker, librarian, stewardess, teacher, housewife, or nurse. Secretly, she had wanted to become a doctor like her father whom she admired so much. But she knew that for a woman to get into medical school at that time required being a brainiac and having impeccably high grades. She possessed neither of those characteristics. So she endured that first year and mustered some enthusiasm about the second year by looking ahead to a highly concentrated patient-care experience during the first semester and hoping for an easy, pain-free assignment to something like obstetrics.

Liz knew that each second-year nursing student was assigned to one patient at a time, tasked with seeing them through the entire hospital experience, from admission to discharge. What could be better than obstetrics? Helping a soon-to-be-mother through admission, labor, the first day with the new baby, and then discharge home? Sure, the idea of difficulties in birth or premature babies crossed her mind, but she felt certain even the tough cases would be manageable, more than outweighed by the good. She even took the unprecedented extra step of requesting this assignment from her supervisor, a no-nonsense, ex-Army nurse.

Instead, Liz was assigned to medical/surgical nursing. Her primary patient was Mrs. Polaski, a former ballerina who had developed advanced peripheral vascular disease. Complications from years of smoking had taken their toll: her circulation was seriously compromised and the patient was to have her lower leg amputated at the knee. Liz was dumbstruck. What could possibly be further from assisting a new baby into the world than watching an amputation of a leg? As Liz tells the story:

> Luckily, my empathic personality kicked into gear. I could feel the suffering Mrs. Polaski was enduring as a former dancer . . . anticipating life without her lower leg. I spent extra time with her and we became close. I knew—I just knew—I could help.

Then came the day of the surgery. This was a big teaching hospital in New York City, where there often can be two dozen or more people in the operating room. Would any of them be as anxious as I was? I was wildly relieved to see that the room was packed with students, interns, residents, and surgeons. My plan of blending in with the back post and becoming invisible seemed feasible after all. Soon, I thought, this nightmare would be over and I could help Mrs. Polaski with her recovery.

Attendants wheeled Mrs. Polaski into the operating room and the anesthesiologist began to sedate her. Once she was "under," the surgery began. More accurately, the sawing began. I zoned out of my body. Then Mrs. Polaski's leg thumped loudly and splashed into the bucket of blood beneath it. With that, I was back! There was an eerie silence and I heard my heart thumping as I watched the head surgeon scan the room. As his laser sharp focus and imperious gaze zeroed in on my post, I suddenly realized it wasn't the post he was looking at. He pointed at me! "Nurse!" he said, "Come here!" With a loud voice inside my head screaming, "NOOOOOOOOO," I obeyed immediately and calmly walked over to the king of the operating room. "Nurse," he said, "take this leg down to Pathology. Before you take it down, be sure you clean it well and put a tag on the toe. She wants the leg buried in her plot."

I remember again leaving my body and hovering above it as though watching a movie. I watched myself pick up the bucket of blood and leg and take it over to the stainless steel table. I watched myself as I washed the leg and put a tag on Mrs. Polaski's big right toe. I wrapped the leg in cloth and gauze as best I knew how. I then saw myself carry the leg to the elevator and push the elevator button. I witnessed as the leg and I stepped into the elevator. I knew that we got off a few floors down, and walked to the pathology lab. I saw myself make sure the people there knew that Mrs. Polaski wanted the leg saved to be buried with her. I watched as I left the pathology lab with blood all over my scrubs. I saw myself walk through the underground tunnel to the nursing school and push the elevator button for the floor where the dean of Cornell Nursing School was. I watched in amazement as I walked into the dean's office—and without any doubt whatsoever, quit nursing school. On the spot.

That ranks right up there with the most dramatic instances of jumping off a cliff. Leg in hand, Liz kicked herself out of nursing and into her future. Certainly, I couldn't have made up the visual of an amputated leg as one of the most powerful catalysts for career and life change. But Liz's story is very real—and is also a cautionary tale. I worked with her and we teased out the many signposts she ignored and the difficulties she added to those first few post-nursing years by not actively planning in advance but just leaping, fueled by emotion. Hers was an overwhelming emotion, but still only an emotion. The good news is that after her abrupt jump off the cliff, she gave herself permission to find the education, career, and work she would love. And that was the beginning of a life she has continuously created with passion and commitment ever since.

But hers wasn't the easiest, quickest, or most straightforward path. For one thing, since she had entered nursing school without making an open, clear evaluation of her priorities, talents, skills, and values, her crisis point—the day of Mrs. Polaski's surgery—came on fast. If I were to work with this young woman today, here's what I'd recommend to Liz before she marched that leg down to Pathology and quit nursing school:

- Get through the day (without the side trip to the dean's office) and then discuss how you were feeling with a trusted friend, family member, or academic advisor.

- Come up with an interim plan to get through the class work and the hospital shifts until you have clarity about your next step.
- Take time to assess your personal values, talents, skills, goals, and priorities.
- Gather information from outside sources about your strengths and weaknesses. This might include a professional assessment (available through the college's career office or online) and asking a few friends and family members for input.
- Begin listing all the projects you've enjoyed working on in school, volunteer activities, hobbies, work, and recreation.
- Minimize exposure to fear-based and negative TV and radio.
- Begin teaching yourself not to follow negative thoughts of doubt or fear about the future.
- Focus on these action steps before determining a more precise plan for the future, whether it turns out to be continuing in nursing or changing to a different field.

These recommendations would require that Liz put in some serious work (made easier with the action steps at the end of this book). Had Liz taken these steps with forethought and care and discussed the issues with her father, who had been paying for her education, chances are good that he would not have withdrawn financial support. Had she approached her father with the assessment she had done and shared with him a proposed plan to work until there was more clarity about a different education and career direction, his reaction would have been less angry and the consequences softer. Perhaps with reasoned discussion, she and her family could have worked together and made the landing much more gentle. She would have then had the time to prepare, mentally and financially, for a jump this big.

That preparation—advance preparation before winding up on a cliff—is part of what this book is all about. Through stories, steps, and Action Items, you will learn how to discover your own right work throughout your life. For now, know that there are many cliffs and many different circumstances; we all face them, and will, multiple times throughout life. There are cliffs that, in the moment, seem to come as complete surprises to the jumpers, who may be at the beginning of their careers (as Liz was), already well established (as Jim, whose story was told in the preface), or somewhere in between (as you may be). There are cliffs that—if you're paying attention—you can anticipate from a distance and for which you can prepare. With the right mindset and the right vision you can prepare for any cliff, even one you didn't expect.

For many people, despite dire news of reductions in head count and changes in the workplace, when the reduction becomes personal (when it's your employer who's downsizing), the change will likely feel as though you are being shoved off the cliff. Maybe you didn't choose this jump, but know that you can land safely. You can even land in a much better spot and ensure that you're ready for any cliffs in the future.

Or what if you've engaged in serial entrepreneurships that haven't panned out? In chapter 3, you'll read about Snorkel Bob, a well-known and now wildly successful serial entrepreneur in Hawaii. As his story demonstrates, sometimes it takes hitting rock bottom before you know what you don't want to do. Then you can observe yourself and choose to make a fresh plan. There are plenty of stories in the papers, in mythology, in biographies, in family lore to reassure you that what may look like failure in the moment can be the door to success, even beyond one's wildest hopes. Years ago, I heard David Pottruck, the former co-CEO of Charles Schwab Company, speak to a group of high school students at Camp Enterprise in San Francisco. This was no ordinary summer camp, but a business camp sponsored by the Rotary Club and designed to teach students how people build businesses. He told the students that after a very successful college career, academically and as a nationally ranked wrestler, he was used to winning—and utterly devastated when he was rejected by each of the fifty-three medical schools to which he had applied. He told the students that his "failure" of not getting into medical school was the catalyst for his getting an MBA and embarking on his fulfilling and highly successful business career. What first seems like a failure can become huge success!

Similarly, think about publishing. Not every would-be writer is published. Of those who are, only a small percentage sell significant numbers of books. Fewer still wind up internationally known. But those who do often had a long road getting there; many gave up in the process. Fans of the Harry Potter series are particularly grateful that a once-unknown author stuck with her dreams and her writing. Many have read how unlikely her success once seemed, given the author's circumstances.

Here's how J. K. Rowling herself described it when she gave the commencement speech at Harvard University in 2008. After sharing how "rock bottom became the solid foundation" upon which she re-built her life, she said that in time, she "stopped pretending to myself that I was anything other than what I was, and began to direct all my energy into finishing the only work that mattered to me."

What she—and the rest of us, children, adults, booksellers, movie-makers, even Disney, which now has a Potter-themed park—gained is remarkable. Rowling's leap, from rock bottom to world fame? How's that for magic? From a distance, it may seem magical, but it demanded all of her inner strength and perseverance. The magic may well have happened because of her commitment: she jumped off the cliff with one big leap, creating an unstoppable commitment that launched one of the biggest multimedia successes in literary history.

You've read about three different types of cliffs and read hints of yet a fourth. What have we so far?

1. Stepping off a cliff spontaneously, in the moment.
2. Being pushed or shoved off a cliff by circumstances or employers.
3. Facing multiple failures, hitting rock bottom, and realizing there's nothing to lose in taking another leap. Sometimes that rock bottom inspires the courage to jump.

And the fourth? It's one I'm partial to and wish I could have advised Liz of in advance. It's one that many people (and probably a high percentage of this book's readers) choose, quite intentionally. The fourth cliff? Making the time to decide on a path and planning next steps before voluntarily leaping off a cliff. Often this involves what I call dual tracking: holding onto your day job while you determine and plan, long-term, for your right work. Or it may mean finding work that pays the most for the least amount of effort as a temporary measure in support of the project of finding your right work. This process—which is carefully explained in *Finding Right Work*—involves objectively assessing your unique talents, skills, values, and current priorities, relative to your work. It is, as you'll discover, a process you may want to return to again and again, as you reach new stages of life and as the world around you changes. Any time you're approaching a leap, the safety net of a continuous income stream can make that leap much more directed and less intimidating, as we'll see in later stories. Whether your safety net comes from savings, from a job that covers your expenses and leaves you with energy to pursue the research, training, or education you may need, or whether it's serious economizing that enables you to dip your toe into higher risk activities, that's all to be determined. And all possible.

No matter which type of cliff you find yourself on and how prepared you feel or don't feel, it's all about embracing change. And, when you take the time to evaluate and to really listen (to yourself and to others), I guarantee you will begin to know which direction to take and how best to take that final step off your cliff. And yes, just like the high dive, it may feel scary—until it feels exhilarating. But if you end up not jumping, and just staying put, realize that you've decided to fail by not even trying. Don't let yourself become one of the people Henry David Thoreau described when he wrote, "Most men lead lives of quiet desperation and go to the grave with the song still in them."

I recently had a discussion with client and friend, Marti Spiegel-man, that further expanded my thoughts on the cliffs that bring us to change. Marti holds a BA from Harvard University in biochemistry, with secondary studies in neurophysiology. She also earned an MFA in graphic design from the Yale School of Art and Architecture and was a practicing graphic designer for twenty years and president of her own design firm. She also trained and mentored in visionary craniosacral work, psychology, and a wide variety of other healing modalities. And now? Marti was named the 2010 Cambridge Registry Executive Professional of the Year for her work with shamanic technologies and evolution of how we do business. You read right: she's a shaman and teacher and founder of Shaman's Light, dedicated to helping leaders "restore their businesses to centers of creation, exchange, and distribution of value for the greater good." From biochemistry to design to shamanism, she knows about change from the inside out. Could Marti have predicted her current profession at the beginning of her career? Maybe not, but she now sees that every piece was important; each change along the way had a purpose that has contributed to where she is now. Marti's has been what she refers to as a "zigzag career," one in which all the pieces have now come into play.

At lunch one day, we talked about cliff jumping and change, those that we've been through ourselves and those that we've helped others through. As Marti puts it, she's using her experience and awareness to help people understand that their significant life experiences—often what we think of as "cliffs"—are really part of people's initiation into the future, into new levels of consciousness. In her work, she helps others "weave the known and the unknown and release into what can be" without fear. In Marti's view, there truly is no reason for fear. What would she have to say about cliffs, and her own fourth cliff in particular?

If you bring your training and consciousness to the current job that you are in, that is exactly where all the doorways are going to become apparent to you. Not from your employer but from your context. So, yes, you earn money. You will do better at the job that you are about to leave. You will make more contacts right where you are earning money. And you will be able to create a platform from which you can launch yourself. It is one movement. It is not "this versus that."

With that change in perception, change becomes less effortful, more freeing.

Marti teaches people how to create lives they love by going within and reconnecting with who they really are. She teaches people the power of their innate creative force and how to access it. She knows and teaches that managing change is an inside job, that managing fear is an inside job. Accessing wisdom is an inside job. As you will see from the stories of those people who have created right work and who are living lives they love, finding right work and living a life you love is an inside job!

Like Marti, a good friend of mine, Diane, is remarkably skilled at staying open, facing change, and making it look easy. Her career has also constantly evolved and evolves still. From the beginning of her emerging career in fashion design after graduating from the Fashion Institute of Technology in New York City to her present roles as executive director of Attitudinal Healing International and global ambassador, author, and entrepreneur in the San Francisco Bay Area, Diane's career trajectory seems nearly as unlikely as the zigzag of Marti's career. Interestingly enough, each aspect of Diane's career evolved from the former stage and—despite the sometimes enormous leaps—felt right to her at every juncture. In the transition from owning an art supply store to owning a fine art gallery in Tiburon, California, the connection was clear. But from supervisor of all TWA flight attendants to the art supply store, or from publishing books to getting her PhD in psychology in her forties, to now? Those seemed like big shifts to me and I'm someone who has spent decades counseling people through change. I asked Diane about the catalyst for her change and her levels of fear when she jumped off of her varied cliffs. A few years ago, she described them to me this way:

> I was never afraid. I knew I couldn't *not* make these changes because I felt like I would suffocate if I didn't. And I was used to it: I always make decisions dead on and all of a sudden. For me, the consequences simply become less important than the doing of it or the going towards something new. In many of my changes, I didn't know exactly what I was going towards, but I did know what I was done with. It was almost like I was finding a new part of me when I left the old part of me behind.

To me, Diane's ease with the jumps from her many cliffs reflected an unstoppable commitment to grow and change and reminded me of a quote I'd read long ago: "In order to get where you want to go, you first have to leave where you are." And sure enough, this was the anonymous quote Diane had posted on her desk early in our friendship. It's still there, by the way. Diane lives her life by it.

From my perspective as a recruiter, coach, and author, as well as from my many years of listening to clients, employees, and candidates relate their work stories, I see consistency amid all of these seemingly disparate cliffs and stories. I've learned that people who have committed to their journey toward right work are always supported by seen and unseen help and experience a tremendous upsurge of serendipity, creative ideas, and high energy. Timely ideas and helpful people magically show up, along with opportunities and even financial help. No need goes unmet when there is the faith that it will come and when fear is supplanted by commitment. Inner guidance is always available when it is requested. Everyone who is committed to finding answers, finds answers. Could it be that when people are in the flow of recognizing who they really are, they have been "initiated," as Marti would say, into a new level of consciousness where their true power to manifest everything they need can be accessed? The reason it happens is far less important than the fact that consistently, for all types of people, in all stages and ages of life, magic does happen via the commitment to discover right work and to begin to live lives they love.

Willingness to change and jump off familiar cliffs is critical for finding right work. Over the years, I've seen that many people in our culture don't give themselves permission to jump and change. Sometimes it's fear of the unknown or a misplaced loyalty to employers. Sometimes they feel they don't deserve to be happier or make more money or have a fuller life. They don't realize that the need to grow and change is a fundamental human need. The need to grow into different work at different stages of life can be a part of this need.

If you want help making the idea of change less frightening, imagine if you were still working in your very first job as a teenager. Or if your first career-track job retained the exact same parameters as that first day, year after year. How can that be good? The reality is that you'll need to face many different cliffs, that what is a good fit at one age, one stage, one place will not always be the right fit for you. Know that finding your right work is also about finding yourself. And with that comes an extraordinary burst of energy, creativity and empowered productivity. Jim, Marti, and Diane are true testaments to that.

Diane wasn't afraid of stepping into the unknown. Neither was Marti. Jim exuded conviction and fearlessness as he took his dramatic leap into the unknown. And Liz? Certainly she was fearful, yet as she leapt off her cliff, her fear of the future was far less than the pain of the present. In the next chapter, "Let Go", we'll see how she—and the rest of us—might diminish those fears and move ahead to become the people we dream of being and discover the work that is right for us. To help put those fears away, realize that, as Marianne Williamson has written so poignantly in *Return to Love*, "Your playing small does not serve the world."

Your commitment must be to discover, to change and grow as you move into the unknown and find answers that you don't yet know you have and uncover opportunities you cannot yet imagine. It sounds like a big order—and it's all manageable. So before your pain of the present becomes bigger than your fear of the future, identify your gifts and passions and determine what your top life priorities currently are relative to work. Spend time assessing those values, innate talents, and abilities and evaluate how closely they align with the work you've chosen. If you are working, pay attention to your strongest emotional reactions and learn what is triggering them. Allow yourself to observe your reactions and reflect on them, rather than being in them and acting on them in haste. Take the time to assess the situation and discuss your frustrations with others, perhaps a trusted friend, family member, or an advisor. Invite other people's perspectives. Don't wait until emotions build and burst to admit to yourself, and then to the rest of the world, that you are in the wrong work. Don't wait until emotions dictate your behavior and you have lost the power of discernment and choice. Don't wait until there are fewer and fewer options to plan. Instead, begin to know who you really are separate from the work or the job you are doing and notice what you no longer want to do in your work and in your life. Begin to know what is most important for you to give and what is most important to get back at this stage of your life. Recognize your biggest gifts and talents and see where your passion is. Understand what values drive your life and spend time writing them all down.

Know that once you jump, you are never alone and without help in your journey. With this book in hand, you have a way to manage the project of your journey to right work. The chapters and the Action Items will help you get there. The Action Items at the end of the book are divided into three categories: outer work, inner work, and outer and inner work together. As with that first jump off the high dive, there are outer conditions you need to check to ensure your safety and success, inner conditions you need to foster to make the leap with confidence and positive energy, and some that are integrally tied together. Whether you undertake the Action Items now, in parallel with reading about the five steps to right work, or as a second phase in reading this book is up to you. You know how you work best. Once you get to the Action Items, realize that there's no one "right" order to them except for this: Get started!

You've jumped! Or at least read about it. If you're feeling shaky about a jump of your own, read this story before either starting the next chapter or dipping a toe into the Action Items at the back of the book.

My friend Dick Buxton uses a powerful image to describe the fear that prevents people from stepping out on the next part of their work and life journey. As he told me, most people are like desert travelers who stop at the first oasis that they see in life and they never leave it. Those few who aren't entirely content with that oasis, who believe that there will be an oasis that has more of what they want and that better suits them, those are the ones who step out onto the desert. They fill up their canteens, pick some dates, and head out to look for another, more abundant oasis. But it's not always easy. Sometimes as they trod along, they spot another oasis, one that looks better from afar. But the closer they get to the oasis, the more it seems to disappear. And all of a sudden it's a mirage, an illusion, not there at all. Maybe it shakes their faith just a bit, but there they are, searching in the desert. What choices are there?

Imagine that they muster the courage to keep looking and the next one is an illusion as well? And the next? What happens then? Sure enough, they race back to that first oasis, rejoin the people who never left, and live (if you call it living) on what's left of the muddy water and old dates. It's a sorry image and, sadly, all too close to reality for many. But, just as there are mirages out there, there are real oases to be found for those who keep looking and believe that they will find them. Those oases are the opportunities that you find once you commit to finding them and are clear about what is important to you and what your priorities, strongest talents and values are. Dick has found many new oases over the years. In doing so, he never trodded or plodded. He trotted, always confident he would find his next even better oasis. In fact, he found a new oasis and introduced a new service in his consulting business as recently as this past year—in his mid-eighties!

You'll read more about Dick Buxton in chapter 3. For now, take a moment to think over any oases in your life, ones you've lingered in and others you may have passed by. If want to increase your momentum and get started on an action item before reading the next chapter, start with getting time on your calendar for your project of finding right work. See the "Make the Time" section in the first set of Action Items at the back of the book. (This is described in "Prepare to Be Prepared," the outer Action Items.)

chapter 2

Let Go

One does not discover new lands without consenting to lose sight of
the shore . . .

ANDRÉ GIDE, FRENCH AUTHOR

Giving yourself time to prepare before a big jump is important. Know that there are always reasons to wait, and if you stand too long waiting to jump, there are consequences. You may be safe, but you might not be effective; you may miss the right time; you may have to step backwards to try again.

You don't want to be standing up there on the edge when a lightning storm rolls in. Or the wind picks up. Despite changes in the world, despite changes in the pool, you do need to take that deep breath and jump—unless you'd really rather climb back down the ladder and not enter the pool at all. That's possible at the swimming pool, but in the work world? Be reasoned about it, be wise, and don't allow fear to talk you into postponing the time when you do leap. If you do, you'll be postponing pleasure and satisfaction you'll wish you'd had sooner, contributions you'll wish you'd made. Trust that leaping is the only way to go and to grow. Have faith that you have been guided to the edge. Know that there will be a pool below. Once you've prepared as best you can, take the leap.

I've been using the image of a jump off the high dive, but take another little leap of imagination and imagine that diving board as a rope swing. Not one with a bench built in, one you sit on, placidly swaying back and forth whiling away the time and admiring the scenery. Instead, picture one more like Tarzan's. But instead of a twisted vine hanging among the treetops, this sturdy rope is fastened to an enormous tree limb that reaches out over a gorgeous expanse of water. You grab the rope as high as you can reach and run with all your might toward the water. If you don't let go at the top of the arc, what happens? Let go a little late or even a little early and you still land in the water, though maybe not in just the perfect, deep spot you'd have preferred. Keep holding on and you could wind up back on the beach to try again. If you don't work up your courage to let go, your arms and your legs may get tired before you get it right. Tired or not, if you don't use the momentum you gain by running and swinging out with the rope, you risk winding up dangling over the water, slipping in when you lose your grip or your arm strength—and what fun is that? Worse, instead of landing in the water or on the beach, you could swing right into the tree.

Why am I bringing up all these images? Do you find yourself picturing the water or the tree? *What you focus on makes all the difference.*

Much as I would have advised Liz to go about her change of career—from nursing student directly into the unknown, with no safety net or support system—differently, I would not have wanted her to hang onto that rope of nursing indefinitely and feel like she was hitting a tree every day of her schooling and then every day of work. She would not have done well getting pounded by her career and she would not have lived the life she dreamed. In the long run, letting go of nursing was absolutely the right thing for her. But could she have made the transition easier on herself by managing her young mind and not reacting so strongly to her experiences during Mrs. Polaski's surgery? Could Liz have made the transition easier by choosing to rein in her emotions so that they didn't kick her off that cliff? Absolutely. But either way, better that she not have joined the ranks of those who stay in wrong work because of the fear of change or the fear of the unknown.

Certainly Liz was not alone; we all face these fears at many different times in our lives. And, given the speed at which technology and the global economy are changing, more and more of us will be jumping more frequently as we learn to weave a tapestry of work unique to ourselves over the course of longer lives.

All too often, those who think they don't know what it is they want to do (when they "grow up" in their "real" jobs) stay in work they found "by accident." They stay in jobs for which they are either not well-suited or that don't use their talents and strengths on any level. Why? Keeping the jobs they have seems less frightening than jumping off the cliff into the unknown. Since they don't know what it is they are searching for or what their talents, priorities, or strongest skills really are, they fear that if they jump, they will go "splat" at the bottom of the pool or ravine. They can't imagine anything else they could do and so can't imagine how they would make a living.

But the "letting go" in this chapter is more than letting go of the fear of jumping and committing to finding your right work. It's also about letting go of needing to know exactly what you do want and what your right work is going to be.

For many people, living in the zone of the unknown is an especially difficult step. What they know seems safer. Perhaps the adage that "the devil you know is better than the devil you don't know" rings in their heads. Particularly given today's world—one in which children grow up with every moment scheduled and supervised, where everyone (or so it seems) is connected to the Internet, to their phones, to their calendars—it should not be surprising that moving toward the unknown can feel daunting. But there's no getting around it: you need to commit yourself to the journey in spite of not knowing the specifics of your destination. The good news is that even if anticipating moving forward feels scary, that does not mean the process has to be scary or even difficult.

Many years ago, I discovered a little book that has had a major impact on my thinking and my life. When I first saw *Love Is Letting Go of Fear*, I was drawn to it like a magnet. I read and re-read it innumerable times. It's no exaggeration to say that the book changed my thinking, which then changed my life—and that its author, Jerry Jampolsky, became a hero of mine.

What was it that first drew me to *Love Is Letting Go of Fear*? I certainly couldn't explain it at the time; I knew only that I felt I had found a precious teaching whose wisdom inspired the courage to change and let go of negative thinking and fears. Looking back on it now, I'm reminded of the Buddhist proverb, "When the student is ready, the teacher arrives." I was in need of and ready for the book's main messages: the importance of letting go of ego and the fear-based behavior that keeps us playing small. The lessons Jerry Jampolsky described so well in *Love Is Letting Go of Fear* were a condensed essence of *A Course in Miracles*, a self-study course for mind and life transformation. Even if I had come across the *Miracles* books at the time, their apparent weightiness (three volumes and a workbook) and strong spiritual nature may well have scared me away. I did, after all, have more than enough reading to do as a German literature major at Columbia University and I wasn't then particularly drawn to self-help or spiritual books. For any outside reading, I needed short and digestible. Jampolsky's book was just the thing.

In all my moves, the book came with me. In time, I read many of his other books, and those that he and his wife, Diane Cirincione, have written together. I was a big fan, but the likelihood of my meeting either of them seemed remote. Years passed and my collection of Jampolsky-Cirincione books grew to fill a sizable portion of a bookshelf in my floating home in Sausalito. One week, the dock's grapevine buzzed with news that was very exciting to me. But was it true? Could it be? One Sunday afternoon, as I walked from my houseboat toward the parking lot, I saw a man loading clothes and boxes into a cart and heading up the dock. I dropped what I was carrying, jettisoned all my normal reserve, and ran toward this new resident, gushing, "Jerry Jampolsky! Is it you? I can't believe I get to meet you. What an honor to meet you! Many, many years ago, your book changed my life—and now we will be living right across the dock from each other!"

Jerry beamed at me with the kindest smile I'd seen, asked if I was "huggable," and gave me one of his well-known bear hugs. That day, a very important person in my life became real to me. What I didn't know at the time was that I would be blessed with the deep gift of friendship from two people whose inspiration and support were a big influence as I expanded more deeply into my own current right work by writing this book. I can't overstate how much Jerry and Diane's books and their personal presence in my life have meant to me. And now that influence extends to you, for surely without theirs and other's support and encouragement, *Finding Right Work* might not yet have been written.

It's only natural that I'd want to include them in this book as I knew there were stories in their lives that would help others along the way. You'll read more about them here; in fact, you've already read a bit about Diane in chapter 1. (It was Diane who transformed herself from fashion designer to author, speaker, and global ambassador and who takes on change with utter fearlessness.) For now, let me tell you one story to underscore the importance of letting go, letting go of fear, of preconceptions, of needing to know at the outset what is right for you.

As it turns out, even Jerry had a long and slightly circuitous road to finding his right work. I knew that Jerry had graduated from Stanford Medical School and became a psychiatrist, had been on the faculty of the University of California Medical Center in San Francisco, and had been a fellow in the American Psychiatric Association. Once we had become friends, he told me that for many years, even in his very successful career as a psychiatrist, he had allowed other people to direct his life. No wonder he was so forceful in telling me, "Do not give your power away for other people to decide what you can or can't do." Jerry's turning point came after reviewing *A Course in Miracles* for a friend. Jerry had been what he called a "self-avowed atheist" and, much to his surprise, the *Miracles* message that love and peace were at the core of every human being became his epiphany for dramatic life change. He realized that human beings were all connected and that once the fear of separation left, what remained was the peace of love. Fear was what kept people from knowing and being who they really were.

Jerry built his life and work on this epiphany and the resulting awareness of oneness with his source transformed his mind and his life. He saw that his concern about his self-image was a big distraction and he began to make a shift as he learned to manage his own mind and ego. He began to not let other people influence his mind anymore and learned to listen to his "inner voice" of wisdom, a voice that— despite (or, perhaps, because of) all his training—he had not known was there. He calls this voice "guidance" and told me that when he's in this zone "there's a higher power coming through me that allows me to be peaceful and feel that I can be unconditionally loving and kind to myself and others; that I can be of service to others. And that's what makes my heart sing. So I chose to do a lot of things since then, things that many people thought were impossible. When I'm in the zone, I believe in myself, and believe in Spirit within. It is a place where there is no fear."

Jerry began to live with a joy and happiness he had never known. He began to dedicate his activity and his life to service to others. He no longer used alcohol to numb his mind. As he told me, the focus of his life as a psychiatrist had been extremely self-absorbed and resulted in alcoholic and workaholic habits. In his fifties, Jerry decided that money would no longer be the top priority in his work, counteracting a pattern he realized had been his way of proving his self-worth. He knew too that his obsession with work was a way he hid from his authentic feelings. He began to be more introspective and, through consistent meditation, began to be able to eliminate his fear through daily access to his guidance. Through that shift, he opened the doors to activities and pursuits that made him enthusiastic about life. In time, he gave up his psychiatric practice and rededicated his life to one of pure service. He founded the Center for Attitudinal Healing and with his wife

Diane co-founded Attitudinal Healing International. In 1982, during the height of the global fear of communist menace, Jerry and Diane founded Children as Teachers of Peace, a program that brought children from the West behind the iron curtain to Russia, to create a way for children of the world to express their feelings, ideas, hopes, fears, and desires for a better world.

By changing his mind and changing his life, Jerry has been a positive influence all over the world for over four decades. His work has been a blessing to thousands of people. His "right work" and lasting career became that of teaching people how to change their minds and heal their hearts, through Attitudinal Healing and through his numerous books. And no matter where he is, or what he is doing, he has continued his practice of *A Course in Miracles* every single day for more than forty years.

Had being an author and speaker been his original career path? Not at all. And, given his history, his career trajectory is even more remarkable. Jerry told me that he had been an awkward, insecure child with learning disabilities who, as he put it, "had flunked kindergarten." Nobody, especially Jerry, believed he would amount to much in life.

In one of our many conversations, he described a childhood moment when he had tried to grasp some kind of dream. "Can anybody can be president?" little Jerry asked his parents. Their response? "Not everybody can be president, Jerry. You can't be president!" But even as a child, Jerry worked from early in the morning until late at night at his parents' food store. Everyone worked hard to keep things going. It was there that, despite all the negative feelings Jerry had for himself, he began to realize that he loved helping people—and that he wanted to go to medical school and become a psychiatrist. As Jerry put it, "Part of the reason was that I wanted to learn more about myself. The fact that my parents gave me the Jewish nickname of 'meshugenah' which meant 'crazy,' had left an impression." Luckily, Jerry had developed a strong work ethic and even though he struggled with reading and writing, he did manage to get into medical school. Jerry told me that in a million years, no one—not any of his professors or peers, neither of his parents, nor Jerry himself—ever could have predicted his future work as a writer and speaker. In fact, in one required English course in college, he failed the exam and wound up with a D minus for the term. The professor didn't mince words, telling Jerry, "I don't know what you are going to do in life, Jampolsky, but for God's sake, don't ever try to write a book!" To date, Jerry has published fifteen books, many of which are long-term best sellers. But it didn't happen right away.

I thought about Jerry's very first book, the book that had changed my own life: *Love Is Letting Go of Fear*. Through it, I began to learn that my thoughts were choices I was making and that my thoughts dictated my experience of the world. Jerry Jampolsky had changed my life and millions of others' lives by writing the books that his college professor told him he couldn't write.

I wondered how many other books have never been written, paintings never painted, businesses never started, ideas never realized, and lives never fulfilled—all because people listened to the voices of parents, teachers, or friends who told them they could not realize their dreams and should not waste time and effort trying. From my decades as a recruiter, I knew a generalized answer to that question: the great majority of people have not even tried to reach their dreams because they were brought up short by other people. Sadly, they listened to other people's opinions and voices over their own. Fortunately, Jerry didn't heed the negative comments from family and teachers about his abilities or those from the medical establishment that for some time considered his work New Age and too far from the mainstream. Through the years, Jerry has stayed on his path, and recently received an award from the American Medical Association acknowledging him as a pioneer in the mind-body healing arena.

Are you afraid of letting go and moving forward, not knowing what is ahead? Let go of that fear. As Jerry and Diane teach, fear is nothing more than a bad dream created by thoughts and experiences from the past projected onto a seemingly unknown future. The present is the only experience that is "real" and our experience of it is the manifestation of past thought projected onto the movie screen of our minds. By changing our awareness and thoughts, we can make our futures very different. As Jerry so succinctly put it, "The fear that people have about changing the way they work may be completely and totally eliminated by healing the mind and recognizing our oneness with one another. When there is integrity between what you are thinking, saying, and doing, there is inner peace."

A sense of inner peace may be a far cry from what you feel as you contemplate leaping into the void and letting go of needing to know your next step. But you might be surprised at how staying open to what is ahead, truly letting go of needing to know—in spite of fear—can reap great rewards, and reap those rewards quickly.

Part of my interviewing process in my present business, EASearch, is to determine who would be the right fit for a very specific position I have been hired to fill. I have all the job parameters, potential areas for growth, and a good understanding of the client's personality, weaknesses, strengths, strategic focus, and company culture. I'm searching for deeply matched support as well as compatible chemistry. Many of the questions in my interviews are directed toward finding out if the candidate has the priorities, values, skills and mindset to match a particular client's needs. If so, the match will surely help to increase the client's productivity and creativity. Beyond the exact skills required for the job, I also look to see if the candidate can commit to increasing levels of responsibility over the years. Sometimes the unspoken task is to tease out how long the candidate would be likely to stay in the job, if hired. My goal is for long-term mutually beneficial relationships in which both parties thrive. And it is not about the one-year guarantee I offer clients; it's about satisfaction for everyone involved. It is emblazoned on my mind that when someone is in right work, their priorities, values, talents, skills, and experience are aligned with the needs and offerings of the work. Long before I started writing this book, the idea of right work was a guiding rule in my career. I wouldn't place people in jobs that I knew were wrong for them; instead, I'd do everything I could to help them in their journey to their right work.

A top executive assistant, Linda Wosskow, was referred to me years ago. Linda had been raised in England and had graduated from secretarial school there. Her experience had been that of high-level support for some years; she was then working as a senior EA at a prestigious consulting firm in San Francisco. On paper, Linda was a "Bingo!" candidate and, even before our first meeting, I was scanning our book of business to see what client might be a match for her.

A high-energy woman with sharp intelligence, Linda arrived right on time for our appointment. Her dress was one of high style and fun. Her eyes sparkled and connected with mine as we said hello. I knew I was going to like this woman. After getting to know her a bit, I directed the interview toward priorities, saying, "Linda, let's take a moment to really understand where you are in your work and what are your life priorities. Priorities shift in life and are critically important in the process of making sure you are in right work. When you think about time commitment, money, meaning, type of industry, location, and other factors, what are your current priorities?"

Linda thought for a moment. Then, the first thing out of her mouth was, "I want to feel fully alive!" She explained, "I have been working for a big company where there is a rigid hierarchy of roles. Support staff are almost invisible." I could see that Linda was beginning to become emotional. I soon learned that she perceived her boss as noncommunicative, disrespectful, and overly demanding; her job had become unbearable. She felt an overwhelming sense of suffocation of her life force. "You know," she said, "I feel as though I have been experiencing a kind of soul abuse."

Soul abuse? That got my attention. What was that all about? I looked closely at Linda, wondering what else was going on. I didn't know her boss, but I did not think that her company was known to have an abusive culture. It was a big consulting firm filled with busy, bright, high achievers. Most of them were overworked and didn't have lots of time for interactions with administrative staff, but Linda was an experienced EA and that should not have surprised her. What was missing in Linda's life? What was the real reason she felt so empty? What work did Linda really want to do that she wasn't now doing?

"Linda," I said, "I want you to listen carefully to my next question. You may even want to close your eyes for a moment." Then, quietly and calmly, I led Linda into my favorite unexpected question, what I thought of as my magic wand question. Before asking that question, I first said, "Now that your eyes are closed, I want you to open your hands in front of you. Imagine that I have a magic wand and I'm now handing it to you. Hold onto it and breathe a moment." After that quiet moment, I said, "Linda, if money were no object, and success was guaranteed," I paused before finishing the question, "what would you be doing in your work life?"

With her eyes closed, Linda slowly repeated part of the question in her lovely British accent, "If money were no object and success was guaranteed," Linda sat up straighter and opened her eyes, "I'd broker Latin musicians!" she said, her eyes glistening with tears.

"Broker Latin musicians?" I asked incredulously. That was an answer I had never heard before and certainly hadn't seen coming. But it couldn't be denied. In saying just those few words, Linda's energy had gone from the low of soul abuse, as she described it, to joyful anticipation as she imagined her deepest dream into being. Years later, when I reinterviewed her for this book, I learned the source of this interest. Then, in that first interview, it was clear to me that Linda needed to act on her dream, so I asked, "Why don't you go do that?"

Linda's eyebrows shot up and fear swept over her face. "How would I do that? How would I make a living?" she asked.

I told her that her skills and experience were so strong that if she created the intention of finding a part-time job while building her company, a part-time job would come along. Linda looked at me for what seemed like a long time. Then . . . "I'm going to do it!" she almost shouted at me. "I'm going to do it!" Oyé Productions had been born.

As an aside to Linda's story, I've used that magic wand question many times over the years. Without exception, people smile at the thought, take a leap of imagination and faith, and hold that invisible, weightless, imaginary wand. Never has anyone refused the wand. Everyone sits taller and more relaxed, happy to have the power to explore possibility, safely. With the wand in hand, they can still the voices of doubt, and strengthen their connection to their own inner wisdom. Sometimes these few moments with the wand are enough to surface long-hidden passions and dreams and give voice to them. Releasing someone of money worries and fear of failure—even just for a few magical moments—can ignite the spark that starts a process of powerful change.

Linda's magic wand got her through what is for some people an unnervingly long time of determining what right work might be. I could tell, just by looking at her, that she knew in her heart and in her gut that brokering Latin musicians was right for her. Once she said it out loud, she had only to come up with a plan and bring her work skills into the task of building a business that was her passion. Linda didn't leave her full-time position right away; instead, she directed her non-work hours into incubating plans for Oyé Productions. Interestingly and quite serendipitously, soon after Linda's declaration of her dream, one of my clients called with a request for a part-time EA. Linda was the very first (and only, as it turned out) person I called. She was perfect for the job, just as it was perfect for her.

As Linda made the switch from full-time to part-time employment, she was faced with plenty of questions from co-workers, friends, and family. She was well prepared for these questions and her enthusiasm was so strong that her quick description of her plans—her statement of intention—sparkled. She explained how she was making time and room in her life to build her dream, Oyé Productions. And, sure enough, she started getting tips and leads, information that helped her grow her new business.

Linda worked part-time at Odyssey Ventures for ten years while she developed and ran her business on the side. As for finances, she lived carefully and always had enough, even on her part-time salary. Her nights and weekends were filled with dancing, networking at clubs, listening to new musicians, advertising for talent, and developing clients. She worked tenaciously to build her network of musicians and proactively built a business that became well known in its field and that boosted her income. She was immersed in what she loved: Latin music. Word got out that Oyé Productions was the place to be registered if you were a salsa musician of any kind in the San Francisco Bay Area. Her network of contacts grew; her two part-time ventures—as Odyssey's EA and Oyé's everything—ebbed and flowed in a vibrant rhythm in which Linda felt fully alive all of the time. What a difference her decision to act on a dream made in her life, in the lives of Latin musicians, and all those who enjoyed them.

What if your heart and gut don't shout out to you right away? What if no answer comes when you ask the magic wand question? There is no one-size-fits-all plan. Letting go of needing to know will help ensure that you keep your view wide enough to encompass possibilities that don't yet come to mind. Possibility thinking requires moving into the unknown and letting new ideas arrive; it requires letting go of needing to know. For that, most people need ways to quiet their minds, calm the voices of doubt, and move forward with confidence into the territory of the unknown. You'll read much more on that in these chapters and in the Action Items later in the book. For now, my advice is simple: Keep open—and go exploring.

Vicki Willock has explored and ventured into new territories throughout her life. She began her career as a statistical typist, became the assistant head of data processing, and wrote code for two years. Then, after a mere three weeks as an executive assistant to the president of an investment fund, the organization agreed to help her return to school for her MBA. Her MBA in hand, she managed one of the organization's funds. Back in the mid-1980s, when there were not many women in the field, Vicki became a senior member of the Bank of America Capital Markets Group specializing in debt and equity private placements. Later, she ran Chase Manhattan's West Coast Corporate Finance operations for over six years, and subsequently established KPMG Peat Marwick's Northwest Corporate Finance operations. The stories of what Vicki has done, the barriers she has broken through over her career, could be a chapter, if not a book, unto themselves.

But here, the focus is on how she went about determining what work she really wanted to do after her very successful management career in banking. So successful that when the bank she worked for closed its California offices, her severance package allowed her to take a year off. She hadn't been happy with the politics in big corporate life, and didn't think she would ever want to return to the work she had been doing. She gave herself that year to explore and to research what work was right for her at this time in life. This is Vicki's story of how she found work she absolutely positively loves.

"I made a list," Vicki explained, "of everything I had ever thought about or wanted to do with my life in work. I wrote it all down. There were fifteen careers in all, including such different possibilities as cruise director, food critic, gourmet food photographer, securities analyst, subordinated debt manager, and health and fitness advisor. With a little research, all pre-Internet, I managed to find someone working in each of the fields." (As she was telling me this I marveled at how much faster this process would be today, with all that the Internet has to offer, including the enormous help that LinkedIn can provide.) Vicki continued, saying, "One by one, I called them up and asked for forty-five minutes to an hour of their time. I explained that I wasn't looking for a job, I just wanted them to tell me about their work. In the interview, I also asked each of those fifteen people for the names of other people in their business. One of my goals was to speak to four to six people in each of the fifteen fields before the year was up."

That seemed like a big task to me, so I asked Vicki how she stayed on track all year with all of those different people. Didn't she get distracted? "No," she said, "I stayed in the mode of interviewing. I was certain that I didn't want to stay in finance anymore, so I was looking carefully for what was next. I thought that the problem, my dissatisfaction, was that I was simply in the wrong industry."

In the process of her research, she realized some important things about herself, which she summarized as follows:

- I love working with people.
- I like to tell the truth.
- I don't like politics; I don't want to report to people who stab other people in the back.
- I want control over my own life.
- I love variety and an ongoing flow of new and different projects.
- I love to raise money and buy or sell things.
- I love thinking out of the box.

In short, Vicki realized what she loved and what she didn't. We love what it is we are good at. The biggest surprise of all was that, after one year and almost 100 interviews with a wide variety of people in fifteen different career categories, she realized she did love the business of selling companies. She also realized that she didn't love working for big corporations. So, she hung out her shingle in San Francisco and started a one-woman business, Willock Partners, which she still runs today. As she told me, "I'm as happy as anyone could be." Vicki's eyes twinkled mischievously as she said, "And, I'm making more money than I thought any girl could ever make!"

Whether I was testing or just being devil's advocate, I went ahead and asked her my magic wand question: "If money were no object, and success was guaranteed what would you be doing with your life?"

Vicki didn't miss a beat: "The exact same thing I'm doing now!" Continuing, Vicki said, "Today is January 15th, I've just had my first closing, and I've made my budget for the year!" Clearly her year of research worked for her. Vicki recognizes that she was very fortunate to have had the financial resources to take so much time off. And she feels strongly that "you can be anything at all you want to be." As she put it, "The process works. Believe it. Focusing time and attention on discovering who you really are works—full-time or part-time."

Vicki once shared with me that she sees looking for right work as being like dating. You have to keep looking and not get discouraged, because the right person might be just around the corner. But know yourself first. So while you are in the mode of letting go of needing to know, remember that determining and finding your right work is typically an unfolding awareness, a journey.

Guidance comes from inside and answers often come from the outside. As a dear friend advises, "Pay attention to your aches and pains; pay attention to your dreams; pay attention to the other ways of knowing. They're all around us, all the time; always available to us." Pay attention to people you meet casually, people you seek out, Internet research, and myriads of other sources. Who knows what sources may pop up, once you are open to it and paying attention?

Let go. Realize that, with your attention directed to it, you will find your right work and you will be guided every step of the way. Realize that first it's important to let go and take the time to know yourself, identify strengths, values, talents, and your own current priorities. Recognize what skills you need to acquire or what education may be helpful to develop those gifts you have. For now, stay open and lead from questions rather than the need for answers.

Remember that staying open truly requires overcoming fear. Despite my well-worn copy of Jerry's book and all spiritual my practice, I have found myself in need of help in banishing fear and moving forward. Years back, amid some major transitions in my life, I felt fragile, frightened, and fearful. And it wasn't without reason: I was emerging from a disastrous financial period after some significant economic downturns, employee betrayals, and partnership troubles, I was rebuilding my new search business, and I was starting to write this book. Fortunately, I had the sense to hire a remarkable coach: Wendy Wallbridge, founder of On Your Mark Coaching. Her strong insights and wisdom led me to the edge of a new cliff. I was afraid. She recognized my fears (despite my adamant denials) and advised me, "Everyone is afraid at one point or another. It is part of growing and changing."

I nodded. Tears came into my eyes and slowly began overflowing down my cheeks. Finally, I confessed, "I am afraid. I'm afraid of so many things right now." They all started pouring out of me. "I'm afraid if I build another company, people will again betray me. I'm afraid that I won't have enough money. I'm afraid that I won't get the clients I need; I'm afraid I won't be able to successfully work the way I want to now. I'm afraid of being so afraid and sometimes, I feel like a big failure."

Wendy quietly asked me three questions in quick succession: "Is it true you want to change your life and create work you love? Is it true that you are ready to create big financial success in your life? Is it true that you are ready to write your book about work?" My answer to each was an emphatic yes! Then she asked, "Is it also true that you are afraid that none of this will happen and you will end up in a trailer park living next door to a woman who wears dirty fuzzy slippers, has curlers in her hair all day long, yells a lot, smokes cigarettes, watches TV night and day, and whose small dog barks incessantly?"

I laughed out loud, for she had obviously identified my worse fears quite well. She then asked, "How big is your fear?" I looked at her, puzzled, so she stood up in front of me and got more specific, saying, "How high off the ground is it compared with me?"

I slowly placed my hand out above the floor. "About three feet tall," I said.

She then reached down, toward the three-foot monster we had described, and said to me, "How about we take her hand and tell her that we are going anyway. Can you bring her with you on your new path? Could you do that?"

My heart skipped a beat. "Yes! I could do that! I could move forward anyway." With that simple gesture and Wendy's questions, I realized I didn't have to wait until I wasn't afraid. I could go anyway!

"One day," she assured me, "you will look down and your little gremlin will be gone. I guarantee it!" With that, I moved forward and stayed open to possibility, knowing that Wendy was right and that what I most feared need not stop me.

Beyond managing fear, another tip for staying open is to be prepared for the questions you will be asked once you begin to go public with your quest for right work. Linda Wosskow was ready with her quick description, "broker Salsa musicians," almost as soon as my magic wand question ("If money were no object and success was guaranteed, what would you be doing with your life?") clarified her dream. Vicki Willock could easily say, "I'm taking a sabbatical to discover my next right work." Chances are your experience falls somewhere in between theirs. But even as you do your research, as you stay open for an Aha! moment, you can prepare the first of a few sentences that may well open up new possibilities for you.

For some people, particularly those not currently employed, the hardest part in the initial phase of discovering right work is answering that ever-present and recurring question of "What do you do?" This comes up daily. It happens in introductions, whether in social or business settings; it even happens in your own head. Having an answer that fits the situation and your circumstances bridges that gap and provides an opening for help from people you meet. So think about, prepare, and practice a one-sentence description of what it is you are doing. You may be taking a sabbatical from your established employment and working as a contractor while you determine your real right work. Understand that this may be the first of many de-scriptions, for the content and purpose of what you tell others will change over time. What might begin as "I'm currently on sabbatical determining what will be my right work" may soon transform into your version of Linda's longer description: "I love Latin music and am starting up my business to broker and encourage Latin musicians in the Bay Area!"

The next chapter will guide you through ways to assess your tal-ents and skills as they now exist. By doing that and then building on your knowledge and clarifying your priorities and values (chapter 4), you can access your deepest inner wisdom (chapter 5) en route to your right work. For now, simply remind yourself to be open and receptive to change as you begin the process of discovering your right work.

Ready to do more before reading the next chapter? See the box "Letting Go" on the following page and the "Create Intention and Begin to Share It" section in the first set of Action Items ("Prepare to Be Prepared," the outer Action Items) at the back of the book.

Letting Go

Letting go of needing to know means letting go of the worry, the push to have the answer right away. In the process, you'll need a way to gather and organize the information that comes your way. You'll find a wealth of guidance on this in the "Establish a System to Manage the Project and Record Your Journey" section in the first set of Action Items ("Prepare to Be Prepared," the outer Action Items) at the back of the book. Here's an abbreviated version, to give you a head start.

Organize your information. Create an easy and comfortable system for documenting your thoughts, experiences, names of people, and resources for yourself.

➤ Make sure that it is a system you'll be consistent in using. You'll need a way to write things down wherever and whenever you have a relevant thought and a way to organize information as you gather it.
  ○ Whether it's a loose-leaf notebook, a laptop computer, a smart phone, or a mini notebook in your pocket and a file drawer at home doesn't matter; the fact that you use it and update it every day does.
  ○ Be sure it's practical for you. Maybe you don't carry a briefcase. You can always take notes in something that fits in your pocket, whether it's a mini notebook or your cell phone.
  ○ Whether you sync your phone and computer or you manually enter your notes into your file system, be sure to make this step part of your day. You want to be able to capture your thoughts, your ideas, your research, your contact information. Every day.
➤ What's the best system for you? Take the time now to select it and begin.
➤ What folders and dividers will you need to keep track of the information that will come to you? Start with sections for professional assessments; assessments from friends, family, and associates; your career autobiography; your mission statement; career brainstorming; your network, both known and developing. As you get closer to your right work, you'll create sections on that field as well.
➤ Set this up and keep it front and center in your workspace at home and in your mind.
➤ One more tip: be sure to label your file. Whatever you choose, whether it's "Creating a Life I Love" or as simple as "Finding My Right Work," putting your intention into print and seeing it will be a constant reminder that reinforces your commitment.

chapter 3

Assess Your Talents and Skills

Your work is to discover your work and then with all your heart give yourself to it.

BUDDHA, HINDU PRINCE GAUTAMA SIDDHARTHA, FOUNDER OF BUDDHISM

The stories of the previous chapter underscored the importance of allowing oneself the time and focus to explore what right work might be. Finding right work requires managing fear and letting go of needing to know. It's a process and one I've helped many people through over the years. I saw a slightly different side of it in 2011, when I gave a workshop that I titled with the question, "Looking for jobs in all the wrong places?" Some of the attendees had been looking for jobs for well over a year. Half of them did not know what they were looking for, only that they didn't want to do what they had been doing. As I heard their stories and offered guidance, I kept thinking of the wisdom of the Delphic oracle: "Know Thyself." Without taking up the course time with Greek mythology and while covering all the topics on the agenda, I also tried to impart the importance of truly knowing oneself, in all aspects of life. That knowledge is critical to discovering right work and it's the heart of this chapter and the next.

On the practical side, "Know Thyself" means you must know how you work most effectively, what makes you thrive, in order to bring your gifts to the world with confidence and in their best form. You must know what your talents and gifts are, what your passion is, what you most want to accomplish at this point in your life. And, just as the other steps toward finding your right work, this is not a once-in-a-lifetime project. Yes, you'll need to know yourself—your talents, strengths, skills (and weaknesses) along with your priorities and values (to be discussed in the next chapter)—throughout life and you'll need to reevaluate many times. By doing this now and making time to assess periodically, you'll be on the right path, whatever your age and circumstances. As a Buddhist proverb puts it, "If we are facing in the right direction, all we have to do is keep on walking." Knowing the right direction requires knowing oneself.

At an age when some people might have walked out the door and opted for early retirement, more and more of us are looking for the next career. We are evaluating where we've been and where the next path should lead. Those thoughts and more were on his mind when a man sat day after day, evaluating his life, reevaluating his life; they were on his mind as he sat, pondering his direction, his past, his future. He had been placed on an official "leave of absence" from his family business. Differences, seemingly irreconcilable, had built walls between family members, between their philosophies of life and business. So there the man sat, shoulders slumped, his notebook before him, at a card table—and a crossroads. Forced to rethink his entire direction in life, he knew that if he were ever going to make a dramatic change, if he were ever going to summon the courage to follow his own star, now was the time to do it.

He set up his card table and chair outside every day. He was away from phones, away from distractions; he was on his own and uninterruptable. Certainly the area around his house made for a scenic spot to think, to assess, and to evaluate his options. He acknowledged his financial situation, which included a great deal of debt. He acknowledged his need for an "exciting new challenge." He took stock of his skills and talents. He admitted not knowing the answer to the question of what to "do" next. Day by day, he continued to set up his card table and chair to think and to dream. He considered new business options.

He saw that the ones on the growing list in front of him were practical and possible and yet, he felt no excitement or connection with his heart when he reflected upon them. He knew that he wanted to commit his heart, sweat, and passion to his next endeavor for the rest of his life. Additionally, he wanted to grow something for his children and his grandchildren.

Amid all this, he found that his mind often returned to his mother's kitchen table where the meals of his youth had been prepared and served. He could almost smell the tomatoes bubbling on the stove as, in his mind's eye, he watched his mother roll out the homemade pasta on the table. Laughter and love filled the kitchen and wine was always at the center of the table. He often thought back on his trips to Europe and the centuries-old wineries he had visited that produced some of the finest wines in the world. He began to acknowledge his deep respect and admiration for these winemakers. Slowly, he began to feel his passion for wanting to create fine wines in the United States. For him, the making of fine wine itself became a metaphor for teaching America his family's Italian values: the love they shared for each other and for good food and wine. Perhaps, at some level, he believed that the better the wine, the more sacred the time. He began to realize that making great wine, sharing great wine, and educating people about great wine would be his life's work and was his deep passion.

His time at his card table by the vineyard was a time of brutal self-reflection. He realized that he had exhibited a terrible temper once too often. He saw that his passion could have the flip side of not listening to others and being insensitive to their needs. Reflecting upon his financial obligations, he realized the need for creating a "prudent" plan right along with a "passionate" plan. As he reflected, day after day, a plan began to emerge; interestingly enough, as it emerged, the phone began to ring with offers from friends to invest with him. Slowly, the alternative ideas fell by the wayside. In time, Robert Mondavi began to know that as painful as it had been to be asked to leave his family's wine business, a new window was opening to his biggest dreams.

At the age of fifty-two, after his time of reflection, Robert Mondavi started his own winery, a company whose name became synonymous with fine wine making, and a company that led and transformed the American wine business. It was Mondavi's commitment to learn from the finest European winemakers that inspired his new company to match and sometimes exceed the quality produced by those who had been making wine for centuries. In time, Robert Mondavi himself became the voice teaching the American public about fine wine and, as a result, Napa Valley landed on the map of the great winemaking regions of the world.

When I met with Robert Mondavi in his beautiful winery in Oakville, California, it was many years after his time at the card table. He was eighty-nine years old. It was clear to me that his life had been, and still was, filled with joy. The enthusiasm in his voice was contagious; his passion for his work, an inspiration. He shared with me some of his heartaches and a lot of his joys: "I feel blessed. So many men and women search and search but never find their passion, their calling, the sense of mission that ignites their hearts and fills their lives with meaning and joy. And so many men and women dream of one day starting their own business, but they lack the necessary skills and resources and they lack a guiding vision of how to create a business and make it successful."

I asked Robert what he would say to someone who had just been laid off from a corporate job, or just starting a career right out of college, or coming back from the military and facing a civilian career quagmire, or to someone who has just retired from a long career. I knew that he had a degree from Stanford in economics and business administration, but I also knew the source of his success ran deeper than that. He laughed and said, "I'd tell them to read my Fifteen Points, the main components for success, from my book, *Harvests of Joy*." I had read his book and knew that his Fifteen Points were full of solid advice that reflected his loving, generous spirit. From "you must have confidence in yourself" to his advice to be "passionate about what you do" and "always stay positive," his words stayed in my memory. Robert continued, "I've never been as smart as many people, but I do have common sense. I've always had faith in myself and in my ability to fol- low through on things. I've always committed to be the best, no matter what it took. I listen to other people, but I do what it is I know to be right. I don't let other people influence me. I continue to learn as much as I can about what it is I'm doing. Knowledge brings self-confidence. And lastly," he said, "you have to live with integrity and speak honestly, from both the heart and the head; not just one or the other! When you create a great style of wine, it takes time and patience; just like a person creating a life, it takes time and patience. I had to travel the world to learn about wine; it took time and it took patience. By looking at the details of wine, we excelled in the wine business. The same may be true with people finding their passion in work. I gave myself permission to create great wines. Then I got busy."

Busy, indeed. Robert Mondavi is now considered one of the most important pioneers of the U.S. wine industry. Beyond being the driv- ing force behind the Robert Mondavi Winery, the first major winery built in Napa Valley, California since Prohibition, Robert and his sec- ond wife, Margrit, were founding supporters of the restoration of the nineteenth-century Napa Valley Opera House and the Oxbow School, which provides grants and instruction to art students in their junior year of high school. Their philanthropy reached well beyond Napa with their 2001 donation to the University of California at Davis, which established the Robert Mondavi Institute for Wine and Food Service there.

Robert died in 2008, at the age of ninety-four. I count myself for- tunate to have known him, done business with his company, partici- pated in several gatherings with him and Margrit where we shared a lovely evening and several extraordinary glasses of wine. I knew that his last years had been lived to the fullest. I was happy to read that a few years before his death, Robert and his younger brother Peter had again made wine together. In 2005, for the first time in the forty years since their feud, they produced one barrel of cabernet blend. The grapes they used were a 50-50 split from both family vineyards; they called the wine "Ancora Una Volta" ("Once Again").

Robert Mondavi's passion will continue to live on in the minds and hearts of Americans who have now been educated and inspired to enjoy fine wines. Had Robert not marched to his own drummer, had he not spent time in reflection at his card table in the vineyards, had he not clearly understood his life priorities relative to work, strengthened his talents and learned to accommodate his weaknesses, had he not had the courage to follow his own dream, imagine what California, the United States, and wine lovers around the world would have missed.

Think of all that Robert Mondavi accomplished after that time of self-reflection in the vineyard. His self-evaluation was critical for him, for identifying his gifts, his passion, and recharging his energy. But don't let the bucolic setting of his evaluation fool you: self-evaluation can be difficult at any age, whether it is at age fifty-two or at age seventeen. While the setting for your self-evaluation may not be as scenic as a Napa Valley vineyard, chances are good that you haven't been removed from your family's business, your financial debt (if any) is considerably smaller than Robert Mondavi's was, and you may have even more years ahead of you than he did.

So now is the time to take stock of yourself, to consciously evaluate your life priorities relative to work at this moment in time, as well as your gifts, talents, strengths, and values. Doing so is key to knowing yourself and will fuel your journey towards your right work. If you're not making progress where you are, if you're not happy in the work you're doing, or if others aren't happy with the work you're doing for them, it's time. If you love your work, but not the workplace, it's time. It's time to take inventory of where you are and where you no longer want to be as a critical step towards finding your right work.

You'll need to take a good look at your priorities as well as your skills and abilities, your strengths, and your weaknesses, inside and out. As Robert Mondavi did, you'll need to take an unbiased inventory of your present life, to look deeply at your current life priorities and passions. You'll need to know (and even analyze) what makes you smile, what makes your heart sing. You'll need to look again at your dreams, some of which may have been long hidden. You'll even need to ask others how they perceive you, what they see as your values, skills, abilities, and weaknesses. The good news is you don't have to do all of this at once or by yourself. Remember: I've walked forty years worth of job seekers through this process. Here, in the chapters and in the Action Items at the end of the book, you've got plenty of practical guidance and help.

Why is it so important to take time to really know your strongest gifts, skills, and talents inside and out? How else can you fully access all that you have to offer and know who you really are now? Imagine that you wake up one day and find yourself manager of a huge store. Common sense tells you that to run it well, you'll need to know your inventory and know the skills and talents of your employees. You'll also need to know who your customers might be, what they need, and how best to reach them. That idea seems obvious to most people and yet the number of people I meet, in my business and outside of it, who aren't accessing their strongest gifts and talents—who don't even know what those gifts and talents are—continues to amaze me. It's as if they're running their own personal store, but with no idea what they can offer to their customers and even less idea of what should go in the front window. That huge gap of wasted potential is what in-spired me to want to help more people discover (or remember) who they really are, and then to find ways to support themselves and con-tribute in their own right work—work that (not coincidentally) will make them happier.

Some people go through life thinking it's not possible, that parts of their lives have to remain separate. So they just endure their work-days. Or they may think (consciously or not) that it's not possible to make money doing what they truly love and are really good at. But why not? Why not tackle the task of self-evaluation and start putting everything together? Why not evaluate, listen to your inner voice, move in the direction of your dreams and create the life you really want? True, it requires courage, time, and inner reflection, but the results can be beyond what you can now imagine. Take small steps at first. Robert Mondavi made the time as a result of having his family's business closed to him—and look what he achieved. He said that he never could have imagined the enormity of his success at the beginning. He took one day at a time, one step at a time. His success is visible proof that tapping into your inner resources, talents and passions truly can release unimagined power and miraculous results.

This evaluation can happen at any time. Imagine the impact if someone undertakes it at an early stage of life. From an early age, Marnie Walker knew that she didn't fit the traditional mold, that she always did things her own way. But as a senior in high school in rural Canada, she hadn't yet reflected upon the advantages or disadvantages of her way or assessed her talents when she suddenly collapsed at cheerleading practice, unable to move. Doctors at the local hospital had no idea what was wrong and transferred her to a teaching hospital in Toronto, many hours from her home. Eventually, she was diagnosed with an extremely rare blood disease and told that it was likely she would die and that if she didn't die, she would never walk again. Years later, Marnie laughed as she told me that, "difficult, problem child" that she was, she decided that she was not ready to die—and that she most certainly would walk again. For four months, she was in a hospital bed, unable to move; four months later, she walked herself out of the hospital and began the rest of her life.

When she did so, she entered a very different life than the one she had left. Given the time in the hospital, the disease, and the side effects of the drugs used in treatment, she was no longer the pretty, athletic girl her friends had known. She was ostracized and continued to be very much alone, even back in her hometown. She knew that she was still the same Marnie, but her childhood friends couldn't see that. She now understood, from firsthand experience, that a person's essence is inside, even if the surface is different or damaged. Tough lessons for a teenager, but lessons that served her very well over the years.

Those months in the hospital, far from family and friends, had given Marnie an enormous amount of time to go within and think about her talents, her life, and her dreams. She knew she would find new friends and create her future on her own terms, from the inside out. As Marnie told me, she learned early in life that "nobody has to accept the status quo. Nobody has to accept the role someone else has made for them." That lesson served her well when, years later, she began to notice that she was less and less excited about her work in business development for a large telecommunications company, a company that had a strong culture of the status quo. She started thinking about starting a business of her own where people would be excited, where they would want to work and where they really would be "thrilled" to be a part of the team. Great idea, but just as Marnie started planting the seeds to start a new business, she found herself in the midst of a divorce. Relying on lessons she had learned as a teenager, she made time to take stock of her life. She made a list of things she'd like to do, things that made her happy, things she knew she was good at. She made a list of what she considered her marketable skills. She made a list of things she didn't like to do or that were frustrating for her. She made a list of the things she really hated doing.

As Marnie put it, "I decided that I was going to stop doing what I hated doing. I decided to try to limit what I have to do that I don't like to do and try to load up the happy quotient of my life." Again, a great idea, but she had children, a mortgage, no savings, and no extra income stream. She certainly could not quit her job. But she believed in the possibility of having her own company and began thinking two to three years out. As far as she was concerned, it was only a matter of waiting for the right time and opportunity to come along. She knew her priorities, values, abilities, and strengths. She knew that she would recognize the right opportunity when it appeared. Meanwhile, she let go of needing to know specifically what that opportunity would be, but she expected to find out. She continued to work hard at her day job and became very involved in the community, volunteering her time and actively networking. When people she knew on school boards mentioned that they were constantly having problems transporting special needs children, and more specifically, what they referred to as "problem children," she paid attention. The boards had hired many different companies and, for various reasons, none of them had worked.

Marnie offered to solve the problem. With nothing to lose, the board agreed to give her a small contract. That satisfied Marnie's entrepreneurial belief of "first get the customers" but she had no company, no buses. What she did have was her full-time job. Quite serendipitously, she was able to compress it into a four-day schedule. She then leased eight buses, hired a manager, and her new company, Student Express, was off and running.

From the outside, starting up a bus company seemed like a major leap. But from Marnie's point of view, it really wasn't. As she explained, "I was sure I could do this because I was also a problem child. I knew that these kids didn't want to be problem children. They weren't trying to be difficult. They just wanted to be able to ride a bus and be understood." Her prerequisite for hiring drivers was that they be able to build healthy relationships with the children. She very consciously and diligently matched each child with the driver she thought most likely to build on each child's strengths and support weaknesses. Whatever the reason, if there wasn't a match, she would move a child to a driver who was a better fit. She wanted the relationship to work for everyone: drivers, children, parents. And it did. How? Marnie used one of the big lessons from her illness as the core vision for Student Express. She inspired her drivers to see those special needs children for who they really were, not who they appeared to be on the outside. A good part of how she did this was by example. Marnie saw her drivers for who they really were and not who they appeared to be. Everyone blossomed.

For over five years, Marnie's work days started at 4 AM as she worked on her bus company in tandem with her day job at the telecommunications company. Her start-up success was nothing short of a miracle. The minimum-wage, part-time, split-shift driver pool cared. Not just about their paychecks, but about the children. Marnie believes that this was the real magic of her company. As she put it, "Because the drivers cared, the kids cared; and all of a sudden, it worked. We transported kids nobody else could, and the company's reputation started to grow."

While Student Express showed a profit right away, it was years before the company could fully support Marnie and her children. Then, once the figures allowed, she quit her day job and the business grew beyond Marnie's imaginings. The company she had started on a shoestring grew to 250 buses and 295 employees; when she sold the business to start her next venture, it was generating over $10 million in revenues.

As it turns out, the awareness and wisdom Marnie had gleaned from the most devastating experience of her life were key for her success in Student Express. She realizes clearly that her very worse experience wound up as the catalyst for a new level of self-awareness that was the foundation for her success in life, in this and subsequent entrepreneurial ventures. Whatever she's doing, Marnie (who is a founding member of Maple Leaf Angels investment group, teaches entrepreneurship at the Schulich School of Business, and owns a managed office center in Toronto) still regularly reevaluates and reassesses. At minimum, she takes one day a year and goes off alone to reflect and to write down what is going well and what isn't, and what needs to be changed in her work and in her personal life. She recognizes that the frenetic pace of modern life too often prevents people from going within for authentic answers about what it is we want to do and who we really are. And she's always grateful that now the time she takes is on her terms, and not enforced by a hospital stay.

The fact that Marnie began this practice early in her life was particularly memorable. In many ways, her story reminded me of my friend Dick Buxton who had, at a very young age, stepped up and taken a very adult stance in the world. When Dick was sixteen years old, his father had an accident that blinded him and left him paralyzed. Shortly after that, the manager of his father's neon sign company cleaned out the bank account and left the city. The employees all quit and the landlord put a padlock on the factory door. Times were worse than tough. Dick and his siblings were going to each be sent to a different relative. Motivated by his passionate desire to keep his family together, he reduced his official schooling to four hours a week and set to work. Dick was already a journeyman electrician and knew how to fix neon signs. Now he went about teaching himself to find business and to run the business. It sounded to me like a formidable task for a teenager to take on, but Dick's attitude is "Life is what you make it." As he told me, over the long term, the worst thing that ever happened to his father wound up being the best thing that ever happened to him. In response to my quizzical expression, he said, "I had to focus on taking care of myself, and I also had to learn how to *not* think about myself and instead think about the family." With that in mind, he took stock of the family's needs and his strengths and weaknesses. He had been shy as a youngster and knew that would not serve him well in the world; he quickly overcame that shyness in the process of drumming up business.

Every night, Dick would drive around his hometown of Long Beach, California with his fourteen-year-old sister and notice what neon signs were burned out. She diligently wrote down addresses and names of companies who clearly needed the services of Buxton Neon. In the morning, Dick would call every company on that list, saying, "This is the service department of Buxton Neon. One of our people noticed your sign was out last night. Can we send someone around to give you an estimate?" Dick got enough appointments so that he could, on a daily basis, make money fixing those neon signs himself. It was a slow start, but after a year and a half, Dick had fifteen employees and five salesmen and had reopened the factory. At seventeen and a half years old, he had rebuilt the company from his bedroom and had successfully kept the family together.

When Dick was eighteen, the U.S. Navy's fleet pulled out of Long Beach. The entire economy of Long Beach imploded and Dick quickly learned the vast difference between accounts receivable and accounts payable. Dick had people to pay and no one was paying him. Nobody could pay their bills and the company's accounts receivable had disappeared with the fleet. He earned $10,000 by working two shifts at another neon company thirty miles away and spending his weekends doing neon repairs on his own in Long Beach. After he paid off all the creditors, he joined the army to get a family allotment for his mother and his four siblings, and so he could take time out to decide on a new career. Each month, he sent all but $10 of his pay to his family so had to limit his recreation to reading several books a week. One of them, *Cash McCall* (later a movie), was a story about a man who founded both a consulting firm and an investment company. The consulting firm referred candidates for acquisition to Cash who would then try to buy the company. Dick decided that he would do the same thing—and he knew he first had to get far more education. He passed GED tests for high school and two-year college level. When he got out of the service, he worked full time as a financial advisor to small business firms and went to college part time (for sixteen years).

Dick's focus on education didn't surprise me, for I have seen his commitment to lifelong learning. When I asked him about it, he responded by saying, "I believe that you can do anything you make up your mind to do. And I'm a seeker; I'm always seeking knowledge. For me, becoming a lifelong seeker is my magic pill."

Over the years and through his careers, Dick trained himself in the skills that he saw were necessary for success. From his early start in the neon sign company, Dick became the youngest sergeant major in the U.S. Army. He led a financial institution in new clients in his first year there; four years later he became one of the youngest executives in their home office. He then built three field organizations. On his way to becoming a top salesman in the insurance industry, Dick taught himself to be a powerful listener by not allowing himself to be distracted by taking notes in meetings. Instead he consciously cultivated a phenomenal memory so that after those meetings, he remembered every single thing that was said. Dick credits his dad with having taught him early in life that Dick *could* train his mind, and he did it well.

In the course of twenty-two years, he acquired the education and experience to focus on his long-term objective of creating a unique private company investment banking firm. He became a pioneer in the development of Employee Stock Ownership Plans and co-founded the ESOP Association of America. Today, over 10 million Americans participate in ESOPs. Dick is now the Chairman of Private Capital Corporation, a firm with clients and associates all over the nation. He's also the co-founder of two private equity groups that have acquired interests in many companies. His firm has created a proprietary management stock ownership plan to attract and retain senior managers who will have skin in the game and a deep interest in the growth of their company. He is a chartered financial consultant and has written two best-selling books: *Lessons in Leadership and Life: Secrets of Eleven Wise Men* and *You've Built a Successful Company, Now What?* His is certainly an impressive list of accomplishments and he has inspired untold numbers of people through the years, all through his creativity and commitment to lifelong learning and involvement. His charismatic nature and inspiring enthusiasm remain stronger than that of many people half his age.

The fact that both Marnie and Dick first began evaluating and reshaping their lives as a result of health crises (Marnie's own and Dick's father's) was not lost on me. Few people allow themselves the time for a full-blown, in-depth review; instead, they find themselves in reactive mode, rather than proactive modes of living. There is little creativity in reactive mode; it's mostly maintenance. By contrast, in proactive mode, there is dreaming, creativity, and unlimited possibility. Since meeting with Marnie, I've paid more attention to this practice of planned reviews and found that many of the most successful people schedule time for life evaluation on a regular basis. Some focus on company goals at the corporate level, at board retreats or company offsites; some do this on the personal level; some are careful to make time for both. One tradition that seems especially positive to me is that of a couple who devote each morning of an annual vacation they take together to evaluate and assess the past year, and modify their long-term plans for the future. They are both away from work and the distractions of daily life, completely able to focus on their big picture together. Their vacation becomes much more than a change of scenery and a rest. This time of self-reflection becomes a deep source of renewal for both of them.

How many people never take that time for introspection and reflection? Over the years, I've seen a lot of them. In my practice as a recruiter, I often have recent graduates referred to me as they finish school and look to begin their careers. I am struck by what seems an almost universal sense of confusion and fear. There have been exceptions, of course, but over the years, the majority of liberal arts or high school graduates appear as though they have been shot out of a cannon and landed in front of my desk. They have had little preparation for the road ahead, they seemed to barely know how to navigate where they then stood. Many recent graduates drew a blank when I asked, "What will people pay you to do? What are your skills, talents, and abilities? What are your strengths and weaknesses? What do you love to do?" Many hadn't really thought about their future work and did not have a clue as to what opportunities might be available for their talents, skills, and abilities—even once they identified them. There was a striking lack of self-awareness despite a huge amount of academic knowledge.

Unless they had experienced a crisis (think of Marnie Walker) or had the good fortune of having a mentor in their lives, many were unprepared. There appeared to be few high school or college courses in self-evaluation and determining one's right work. It felt to me as though there is just the fantasy that after their formal education, work will appear—with no conversation about "right work" or "wrong work." Many end up in jobs similar to what their parents do, since that is all they know. Those fortunate few who felt a calling early on (often in specialized professions such as law, architecture, and medicine) may have been marginally better prepared, but many times they too simply followed in footsteps of parents and acquiesced to unspoken expectations that they carry the torch forward.

I always felt sadness at what I knew would be a long bumpy road on the journey to right work (or any work) for many of these graduates. Many times, people took jobs and then discovered, in the doing, what it was they didn't want to do. This painful and unpleasant experience—repeated numerous times—would eventually bring them closer to knowing what it was they did want to do, but at the expense of lots of time flying by. Self-evaluation, done early on and repeated as needed, would have ultimately saved them a lot of time and brought them greater rewards. As I worked with these recent graduates, I could hear an echo of the voice of my Quaker grandmother, Edie, telling me about the lines in heaven.

When I was very young and frustrated because I couldn't do something as easily as my older brother or younger sisters, my Grandma Edie would gently explain: "There are lines in heaven that you stand in before you are born. Each line is for a certain ability, or attribute, or talent. You cannot possibly stand in every line. There isn't time." This lesson alone would have been a lot for me to absorb, impatient girl that I was. But she continued, "So find out which lines you did stand in. Then you'll see what your own special gifts are. Those gifts are God's gift to you. What you do with those gifts is your gift back to God. Your only real job in this life," she would say, "is to develop those gifts and give them back to the world." Grandma Edie believed, as do I, that if we develop our talents and passion, and if we give our gifts to the world, we find lasting happiness and the world becomes a much richer place for our having lived. Thanks to her lessons and a wide variety of other teachers along the way, I am using my special gifts more and more in my work and in my life. I know that finding my right work had everything to do with remembering those lines in heaven.

As a recruiter and entrepreneur, I've relied on many traits that my grandmother would have said that I picked up early from those lines. I have an easy way with people, I love to connect and help people, I have an empathic personality with strong intuition, and I'm a good communicator. I have a passion for lifelong learning, and have always learned the latest technologies for my field. For any service provider in today's world, constantly reinventing the depth and breadth of your work and expanding your network are key. This means staying current with technology and fully utilizing today's networking sites (such as LinkedIn and Facebook) and staying open to new developments for tomorrow. These skills and interests are just as important as the ability to start a conversation with someone—in line, at a conference, en route to a meeting, on vacation, anywhere and anytime—something that comes easily to me and seems as natural and vital as breathing. I once had three floors' worth of time in a high-rise elevator to introduce myself to Walter Shorenstein, a major commercial real estate developer in San Francisco. As he was leaving the elevator with my card in his hand, he turned and asked, "What did you say your name was?" Once I said my name, he said, "Well, Leni Miller, I'll give your card to the ladies in personnel!" An hour later, a woman in personnel called me; the upshot was that The Shorenstein Company became a significant client of mine for many years.

This natural comfort I have with all kinds of people has enabled me to network more or less nonstop. To me, it's not work; it's fun. My grown daughter, Abby, still remembers reaching up to hold onto my hand in airport lines as I chatted with strangers who would sometimes become clients. Given the nature of my business, the fact that I easily engage with people, have a tenacious and resilient personality, a high level of patience, and a well-developed sense of humor have been gifts critical for

55

success in search and recruiting. Well-organized and well-planned deals will fall apart, clients and candidates will change their minds, and humans will do that thing they do best: behave unpredictably. Each search is new and has a different set of challenges; I love the constant newness of each search. I have a mind that thrives on short-term projects and I do well when I can see the beginning, middle, and end.

The lines in heaven we don't stand in are important to know too. I created a very successful company, McCall Staffing, with a woman who had stood in many lines I hadn't, just as I had stood in lines she hadn't. Once I sold my half of that company and was out on my own, I fully realized how valuable Pegi Wheatley's contribution had been to the success of the whole. She was brilliant at planning for the ups and downs of economic cycles and extremely careful to stay on budget. I wasn't good at either and the lessons I had to learn as a result were expensive on many levels. I have since created a business with support for my weaknesses: I have a strong financial advisor and CPA. I keep my overhead as low as possible and I maintain a streamlined company that requires less financial administration than one with many employees. Our weaknesses don't really change, but we can work around them and support them once we've admitted what they are.

Whether you are looking for a job or an opportunity to create your own way of working, knowing your strengths and weaknesses, your abilities and skills relative to your priorities in life builds self-awareness and confidence that become unstoppable. What lines in heaven did you stand in? Which lines did you miss? There's nothing to be embarrassed about. Nobody can stand in all the lines.

When Warren Buffett was speaking with Bill Gates to a group of MBA students at the University of Washington in Seattle, he was asked what had been the biggest lesson he had learned in life and in business. Without missing a beat, Buffett answered: "Just because you are really good at one thing, don't assume you'll be really good at everything."

How can you know what you are good at and where you don't excel? Ask your spouse, your parents, your coworkers, your friends.

In addition, there are hundreds of strong professional assessments out there. DISC, an assessment tool that classifies four aspects of behavior (dominance, influence, steadiness, and compliance) is used frequently. I have used Profiles International, which I had customized to my specialty area. Myers-Briggs is one of the oldest and best-established assessments in the world. Most CEOs know their Myers-Briggs type as easily as they know their body weight. CEOs generally know which lines they stood in and which lines they didn't. And the successful ones make a point of hiring executive teams filled with talented people who stood in the lines they missed. The Enneagram is another methodology to understanding the personality and has been around for thousands of years, remaining uncanny in its accuracy.

Know your strengths—your gifts—and adapt for your weaknesses. Specific ways to assess your strengths and weaknesses are set forth in the Action Items. As you'll see, the more information you can gather from a wide range of sources, the better. While it might be tempting, for instance, to ask for assessments only from those who are most likely to accentuate the positive, there's everything to be learned about any weaknesses or gaps you may have. Many of us are not aware of our own gaps. To get the most useful information, be sure to extend your request for assessments to a broad range of people and encourage them to be completely candid. Remember, you're looking for strengths and weaknesses, praise and criticism. The reality is that any "negative" reports may be enormously helpful in the long run.

In my experience interviewing candidates and coaching people in right work, there is typically a correspondence between the reports from friends, family, coworkers, and others and self-reports (such as the career autobiography). These results tend to be very consistent among themselves and when compared to outside assessments. But there are no guarantees. Be sure to pay close attention to all the information that comes in. Stay alert to anything that seems to be outside of the range of most results or that seems to ring false. Disparities between your self-image and how others experience you may be particularly telling. If you think you know what you love doing and you're good at but others disagree, pay attention. It could be that you aren't working well with others or it could be that you aren't truly accessing your strongest gifts. Dig deeper to discover who you really are. As you're preparing your autobiography—taking notes on projects and work you've loved, general and specific areas of interest, types of work and workplaces—be aware of your energy level and enthusiasm. If your energy is low when you think of certain work, don't worry about why, simply pay attention to what does make your energy start climbing. When I think about writing my book and talking about right work, my energy is very high. When I think of reading financial statements, my energy hits the ground. These are accurate reflections of lines I stood in and a line I didn't.

Granted, my grandmother's words still echo in my brain, but I'm never surprised that when people have done their evaluations, they see that their strengths and the activities that make them happy, that energize them, often reflect traits they had as children, and activities that might be seen as the childhood version of their current pursuits, passions, and evolving right work. Sometimes preparing their career autobiographies reminds people what it is they truly love and what their priorities are, past and present. That's why in coaching people as they search for right work, I get people started on their autobiographies right away. By reflecting on past work, they often rediscover what it is they loved about some jobs or work and what they didn't like. They often see that their priorities have shifted throughout life. When my daughter was small, time was a more important priority to me than money. When she was in college, money became more important than time. The better you know yourself and know your gifts, priorities, and values, the faster right work comes along.

What if you love snorkeling? If you do, and have been to Hawaii, chances are you've heard of Snorkel Bob. When I first saw his brochure many years ago, I giggled at the picture of a tuxedo-clad young man submerged in water, breathing through snorkeling gear. The headline proclaimed: "Snorkel Bob Cares! Snorkel Bob loved snorkeling so much that he missed his senior prom to snorkel!" I tucked the brochure away in a journal, thinking this was a man with a passion for his work. This was a man, I thought, who had found work he loved.

The years passed. Many of them. As I began to gather material for this book, my mind returned to that brochure's image, and I thought, what a wonderful person for my book on finding right work! Where was Snorkel Bob today? Was there really a Snorkel Bob? Or was Snorkel Bob a creation of some advertising department? I searched the Internet and up he came! The company was still there and its website included a picture of Bob. He was a little older, but still smiling with great enthusiasm for snorkeling and for his company. The text of the website began, "Snorkel Bob was born on Maui a long time ago. He first snorkeled at the amazing age of four, and he says now that he knew even then, 'I wanted to snorkel again. I still can't get enough.'"

As the website described, Bob's snorkeling through his formative and teen years was seen by some as a hobby, a phase he would outgrow in time. But when Bob chose to forego all other sports to devote his time to snorkeling and eventually skipped his senior prom because of excellent conditions for a night snorkel at La Perouse Bay (an area for advanced snorkelers), his parents and teachers feared an obsession. But Bob knew better and transformed himself into Snorkel Bob, with the motto of "I want to bring snorkeling to the people." And, sure enough, it appeared as though he had been doing so, and for many years.

I scanned to the bottom of the website. My heart picked up a beat when I read "Contact Snorkel Bob." Well, that could still be just the marketing people, I thought. I called, and the voice on the message tape said: "This is Snorkel Bob. Thank you for calling. I can't answer the phone right now but I, Snorkel Bob, care about your call. Leave a message." I was thrilled. Of course, I realized that there still might not be a "real" Snorkel Bob. After all, the website had also mentioned that Bob's parents had him see a psychiatrist named Dr. Fischimull; when I thought about it, this wafted of a joke (Fish, I mull?). Still, I was closer than ever to finding out. I left a lengthy voicemail explaining the nature of my book project and the reason for my call.

Days passed. No call from Snorkel Bob. Then, one Saturday afternoon, my cell phone rang. "Leni Miller," I said, "May I help you?"

"Hi Leni! This is Snorkel Bob!"

"Oh my!" I squeaked. "Is it really? You really exist? How wonderful!" I told Snorkel Bob more about my book and that I wanted to share real life stories of people who had created right work so that their stories would, in turn, inspire others. Did Snorkel Bob love his work? Would he share his story? Does he ever come to the mainland?

"Would you like to meet me at Jack London Square, in Oakland, on Sunday?" he asked. He was here! Perfect! Synchronicity at its best! Magic! The appointed time to meet arrived. I walked into the restaurant and recognized Bob right away—even without the snorkel gear. He introduced himself as Robert, and after hearing more about the project, he took a moment to think. Over the next four hours, I listened raptly to the story of his life. It turns out that Snorkel Bob's path hadn't been as direct as his old brochure implied. Not by a long shot.

The biggest surprise, I soon learned, was that Robert's primary passion had been fiction writing. As my mind flashed back to the creativity of his brochure, he told me that right out of college, he went to Hilton Head, worked on a shrimp boat, and wrote for the *Savannah Morning News*. As he put it, "It wasn't fiction, but it was a learning process, and the money didn't follow!" At what was then the going rate of 20 cents an inch, it's no wonder. But he kept writing and his first novel was, he told me, taken "by a really top agent." Unfortunately, he said, "Right before she had sold it, she killed herself." Nonetheless, he kept writing books—and kept getting rejections. Robert told me of failed businesses, natural disasters and other challenges of the practical world, and how he took refuge in writing. I wondered how had he maintained his cheerful demeanor—and how he got back to snorkeling.

Years ago, he traveled to Hawaii—not for sun and fun but to compare notes with a kindred soul, to see how they might, as he put it, "rub two nickels together and come up with twelve cents." He and his friend somehow succeeded in transferring the correct number of dollars from a lender to a California boat owner to put the boat in the water, bound for Hawaii with them at the helm. "It was so perfect, raking in thirty grand a month, staying oblivious to expenses at thirty-five grand." When the vessel got beached in a storm, another struggle ensued with the lender. "We got out with our shirts on, but barely. I felt shipwrecked on a tropical island."

Robert was careful to point out that he did not then immediately or serendipitously rediscover snorkeling as a true love that led to money. Instead, he went to California. It was on a phone call with a friend back on Maui that he "got the question: 'Why don't you come home?'" So he returned to Maui, an island known for healing, with no plan—but knowing that he "wanted to stay in Hawaii and didn't really need so much money to do that."

On Maui he watched tourists rent snorkel gear day after day. "Back then, in 1985, you could only rent gear by the day. Most people came to Hawaii for a week or more. Beyond that, the gear available was cheap, worn and dirty. I recognized a need. They needed gear; I needed rent money and a bag of groceries every few days. I was nearly broke, but I had an American Express card that had room on it. I used it to buy some snorkel gear and print a brochure." He rented his gear by the week for $10.

His venture into renting snorkel equipment was different from all his prior ventures: he did not know it would work and did not strive to make it work. As it happened, the demand for clean, quality snorkel gear was huge. Robert explained, "Even the word, snorkel, sounded comical to most people—yet they craved it. And I felt responsible. The name Snorkel Bob came as a spontaneous afterthought from an admirer, and it stuck. Another fan muttered, 'Snorkel Bob cares.' Maybe I did. From the first, success was never around the corner or a few bucks away. It was a white-knuckle ride, hanging on and staying ahead of demand." That was the beginning. With success and stability in the material world, a snorkel executive could then turn his attention to stability in the reef world.

Robert had always felt an affinity for fish and reefs and "felt blessed by Neptune—not because I was a special kind of guy, but because we had work to do. I had an assignment. The money would cover expenses. It used to bother me that I hadn't made money with writing—yet there I was, hand-over-fisting moolah in a business based on its compelling narrative. If you do what you love, the money may not follow. But you will surely love it."

That concept may seem impractical in making ends meet, but it worked. With the money he made from renting snorkel gear, he started a foundation that now underwrites reef conservation projects around the world and especially in Hawaii. Beneficiaries include the Sea Shepherd Conservation Society, where he's on the board of advisors. The Snorkel Bob Foundation led legislative campaigns to ban the aquarium trade in Hawaii. It was also crucial in a coalition formed to protect the Northwestern Hawaiian Islands Papahānaumokuākea Marine Monument. Then came monk seal protection; then litigation to stop expansion of the Hawaii long-line swordfish fishery, which would have allowed triple the incidental "take" on loggerhead, giant leatherback, and hawksbill sea turtles. The Snorkel Bob Foundation and Robert Wintner are now known in Hawaii tourism and business for caring and for giving a voice to marine mammals, turtles, reefs and reef citizens.

"It's a long march. We have no choice but to take the next step," Robert said. "I discovered a mystical realm that I love, and so do most other people. Markets are more complex than ever, but the natural world is very much in need, and much of humanity feels helpless in mitigating that need. Nobody knows what might work, but anybody can know what feels good, what's fun, what others might want to share. I have three reef photo books out now, and I don't consider myself a photo technician by any means. I simply get out there and get calm and see who Neptune sends my way for a family portrait. I think the only formula for success is to have lively feet, smiling eyes and a willingness to give so much that you may develop support for your endeavors."

Robert spent years and energy focused on making money. It wasn't until he set winning aside to better listen to that "still small voice within" that his genuine success—financial as well as soul-level fulfillment—began. Robert told me, "The money helps you do what you love, but it's not required. As my old partner in the charter trade often advised, 'You better start having fun, Bobby. You're gonna be dead a long time.' I don't know if I agree with him entirely, but I do take his point." Robert also believes that "retirement should be a time when you can stop doing what you don't want to do." But how much better to create a life, as he has, in which you do what you love and never want to retire!

As Snorkel Bob's story illustrates multiple times over, doing what you love within the context of providing a service to people and really caring about them is a powerful way of customizing individual right work. As he put it, "The snorkel business seemed good at the time and ended up working out. I had the right combination of business smarts, snorkel smarts, and spiritual connections. Call it timing, with a little help from my friends." To my mind, it's help that he recognized by being open to it when it came along.

A byproduct of his service to others is an income stream that now supports his passion for saving the fish of the world. Who knows how many millions of fish and other marine creatures, including the coral itself, may well be saved by these efforts? Robert's contribution to tourists supports him and his passions in an all-around great life. His passion for writing is stronger than ever. As Snorkel Bob, he writes guidebooks to Hawaii and its waters; as Robert Wintner, he writes fiction—and the money takes care of itself.

I wondered what else Snorkel Bob might have contributed if, at the beginning of his career, he had "given himself permission" to discover work he loved. What if he had begun his career with permission to find his "appointment" much earlier on? Better still, what if as a kindergartner, Robert had been told that he had a special gift and that his job was to discover and use that gift and give it back to the world? What if he had learned in school to pay attention to what he was naturally good at and create the intention of discovering and strengthening his talents? What if his teachers continued to support the journey of going within and noticing his gifts so that those innate talents became stronger and stronger over the years? Might he have settled in Hawaii sooner? Might his actions in those years have made even more tourists happy with weekly snorkeling gear prices and, by interesting even more people in our underwater world, saved even more reefs and more fish? Snorkel Bob told me that his Jewish mother once said to him, "Bob! Stick with snorkeling! It's the only thing you've ever been successful at!" Could sustainable success be connected to being your gift in your life? His mother thinks so and so do I!

Snorkel Bob, Dick Buxton, Marnie Walker, and Robert Mondavi: very different individuals in different parts of the world and within their work. But read between the lines in their stories and you'll see significant parallels. They each changed direction and found ways to provide services that reflected their values and used their gifts. They put their skills to use in ways they had not anticipated when they were starting out in the work world. With self-awareness came commitment, with commitment emerged guidance, from guidance came passion, and with passion, they discovered their right work, which generated the money they wanted and needed, and then some. As a bigger benefit, they wound up helping others in lasting ways. And, not coincidentally, their work was in line with their priorities and values, the next chapter's topic.

There are many ways to assess your talents and strengths, and ultimately you'll want to use them all. There's a lot of information to be gathered, bit by bit, some through self-reflection and some by enlisting others. For now, focus on what you know about yourself and what you love to do (work related and not). This is one aspect of the information you'll gather as you complete the Action Items in the back of the book.

Gather Information About Yourself

Research and glean information about your beliefs, priorities, strengths and weaknesses. Start with what you know for certain about yourself. Your goal is fact finding: you want to gather information about yourself from more effective self reflection. If you find yourself reacting emotionally or physically to any of the questions, take note of that and write a quick note about your reactions as a reminder.

Volunteer experiences. Think of volunteer activities, of all kinds, in which you've been involved over the years. List them all and take note of what was meaningful to you and what was it you enjoyed about them. Be as specific as possible.

> ➤ Are there any volunteer activities that you always remember? What makes them memorable?
> ➤ Are there any volunteer activities that you've wanted to do, or hope to devote more time to at some point in your life?

Hobbies. List your hobbies and interests. Include what you are active in today, in earlier years, and even hobbies you might like to begin. For each, think about (and write down) what draws you to them.

This is just one portion of the detailed steps involved in drafting your autobiography. If you're inspired to do more now, flip back to the complete section "Gather Information about Yourself" in the first set of Action Items at the back of the book ("Prepare to Be Prepared," the outer Action Items). There, you'll add in information from family, friends, colleagues, even former employers. You'll also get another perspective from professional assessments, whether in person, online, or through books. It's all relevant to assessing your talents and skills.

chapter 4

Identify Your Priorities and Values

There are three things extremely hard: steel, a diamond, and to know one's self.

BENJAMIN FRANKLIN, AMERICAN AUTHOR, SCIENTIST, POLITICAL THEORIST

The previous chapter and this chapter focus on helping you tease out the markers that point the way to your right work. Your skills and talents, as well as the skills you may yet develop through your interests, are just one part of the equation; another relates to your priorities and values, and what you view as most important for you in this particular phase of your life. Values tend to remain consistent over time, but your priorities will certainly change.

And, yes, in order to be sure you stay on your right track, that means you will need to periodically revisit the concept of right work, and compare your current priorities with what it is you are now doing and how you are spending your time both in and out of work. If, early on, you establish a practice of identifying your current priorities on a consistent basis, you will keep yourself from losing time (and energy) by staying in work that doesn't fill your present needs. Even without those personal evaluations, you may get a correction—a cosmic boot—perhaps from an employer, a change in the economy, or family circumstances that will demand that you steer yourself in a new direction.

In contrast to Snorkel Bob, who tried out many different liveli-hoods before hitting upon work that enabled him to help others while paying him so well that he can contribute to causes dear to his heart, some have paths that are much more direct. But many fall somewhere in between.

Not many years after he graduated from the University of Penn-sylvania, Allison Rouse was being paid an amount he described as "a fortune," enough that just one commission check from his job in soft-ware sales to university admissions offices enabled him to pay off his student loans. Given the circumstances under which Allison grew up, that size check and his ability to erase his large debt so quickly were quite remarkable. Allison's success in sales, however, was easy to pre-dict: he has a charismatic personality and a natural ability to grasp situations and concepts quickly. He inspires those around him to want to come with him on whatever journey he is on. That he landed the job and did so well in it is in large part a testament to the values that his mother brought to raising her family, values that he carries on and lives by.

The youngest of seven children, Allison grew up in the projects in New York, living in three different neighborhoods in Harlem and the South Bronx. For many years, his family's home was in the tallest of a five-building New York Housing Authority complex. Drug dealers stood on almost all corners and many boys from his old neighborhood ended up with multiple stays on "The Rock," as they referred to Riker's Island prison in New York City. How had Allison been inspired to stay out of trouble, stay in school, and go to college? Allison's two-word answer? "My mother!"

Allison's mother, Bernice Rouse, raised four of her seven children alone, supporting them by working two jobs, one as a cashier at the Grand Union supermarket. She set high standards for the family, in-cluding that of personal self-reliance, from an early age. A strong work ethic was high on Bernice's list of values. She emphasized, in action and word, the ability and importance of sticking with something and working hard to achieve a goal. Bernice had immigrated to New York City in 1945 from the island of St. Thomas, where her father had been a school's headmaster. She deeply valued education, made it a priority, and found ways to send her youngest five children to private schools.

Bernice had been the catalyst for securing full scholarships to Riverdale Country School, a leading independent school, for Allison and his sister Stacey. To get there, Allison and Stacey took two trains and a bus from the south Bronx to the north Bronx and then home again—ninety minutes each way, every single school day. By car, the trip would have been thirty minutes each way. Was it worth it? Allison assured me it was, and for many reasons. At Riverdale, he began to be mentored and supported by people from a different world. An African American, Allison noticed quickly that African American students counted for less than 10 percent of his class and that minority students in total accounted for perhaps 15 to 20 percent of the school at large. Teachers and students alike supported Allison's academic and athletic endeavors and he blossomed, excelling both in class and as a three-sport varsity athlete. He developed friendships across the school; many of those students' parents also mentored Allison. People reached out to Allison, believed in him, and guided him to believe in himself in a larger context of what life could be. They showed Allison the way into an expanded world of academic, cultural, and financial possibilities. Whether it was learning to eat Chinese food with chopsticks, spending hours reading the Sunday *New York Times*, or traveling to Europe and seeing works in the Louvre that he had studied at Riverdale, Allison burst out of the confines of his neighborhood culture.

He learned not just to survive but to thrive in mainstream America, as well as in the broader, more global culture. Allison's education at Riverdale was not only about knowledge; it was also about becoming aware and learning from the wisdom of others. He was mentored by people who were already living financially prosperous, fulfilled, and meaningful lives. These people gave of their time and shared their life lessons and the practices they had taken on their journeys to right work. Allison began to grow the connection to his own innate wisdom and natural talents; he began to see the possibility of emulating and living a life beyond the bounds of racial programming as described in The *Mis-Education of the Negro* by Carter G. Woodson, which he had read as a junior at Riverdale and continues to recommend in his work today.

In his years at Riverdale and beyond, Allison learned that the most successful people he knew—friends, acquaintances, academics, business people, athletic coaches, and others in the Riverdale community—were those who generously helped others. Given that experience and his mother's teachings, it wasn't long before his early, enormously lucrative sales job simply did not feel like the right fit. Even though the sales side came easily to him, and the software product he sold was extremely useful, the job itself began to feel empty to him. Yes, he was helping educators reach different sectors and streamline their admissions process, but was that enough? More importantly, was that how he could best contribute his talents and give back to the world?

When he left the software company and took a new job at half of his most recent salary many of his associates, friends, and family thought he had lost his mind. They knew he had been in admissions before: his first two jobs after college had been as regional director of undergraduate admissions the University of Pennsylvania and then in the MBA admissions office at the Stanford Graduate School of Business. What they didn't immediately realize was that Allison had learned that for him, the hefty paycheck wasn't enough: he wasn't working for money alone. With that knowledge, and understanding that in his new job, helping others with their educations as the director of the western regional admissions office for the University of Pennsylvania, his career change made perfect sense.

He had also realized that he needed to help others, to "pay it forward," to grow his own feeling of fulfillment in his work. As Allison told me, "You have to slow down enough in the world to figure out your passion, and then when you find it, everything will fall into place. My passion is paying it forward and helping others the way I was helped. You can't always do everything you want, but you can learn what is most important. What I learned from my sales job was two-fold: I learned how to listen better to be more responsive to others and I learned that I need to 'do good' in my work. I learned that I need that feeling of being able to help someone where they are. I didn't get that feeling in sales; in sales I felt I was being judged by the product I sold."

As he moved forward on the road of his life, Allison habitually shared information and resources with other people who needed help. His motto became "Pay it forward" so that if you are given something—some advantage, some lesson, some help—you pay it back, you make your contribution by helping someone else. The idea echoed what my Quaker grandmother, Grandma Edie, would say when I'd ask her how I could ever repay her for all of the help, love, and support she so generously gave to me as a child: "Pass it on," she'd say, "Pass it on."

But Allison soon realized that he had changed and outgrown this new job. He was paying it forward, but he felt he was working at less than 60 percent of his capacity and that much of his work was in areas of his weakness rather than his strength. Not surprisingly, his enthusiasm for the job waned. Allison made the decision to be open to other job opportunities—without any idea of what would be next. He knew what his values, priorities, talents and weaknesses were. He also had complete faith that the right job would appear and that he would recognize it.

One day, Allison's niece Nicole asked him to have a conversation with her college advisor at a KIPP school (the acronym KIPP stands for "Knowledge Is Power Program"). KIPP schools are free, open-enrollment, college-preparatory public schools in what are called under-resourced communities. Allison was so impressed with Nicole's experience at her school and the fact that the middle school had a college advisor that he researched the organization, learning that KIPP charter schools are having great success in educating children in the poorest of America's neighborhoods. Many of their students might not have otherwise finished high school, let alone had aspirations for college; instead, KIPP graduates are going on to college, including a number of them in the Ivy League. Added to what Allison had learned through his niece's request, the information on the Web made clear to him that KIPP's mission resonated deeply with his values and priorities. As he was researching KIPP on the Web, Allison saw that there was a newly posted job that perfectly matched his experience, skills, and abilities. Serendipity? Coincidence? Allison applied, got the job and started recruiting leaders for KIPP, excellent teachers to serve as founders of new KIPP schools. Being the nationwide director of recruitment and selection for the KIPP Foundation was, as Allison described it then, "the hardest job I ever had." He was actively involved with the communities KIPP served, with creating systems for recruiting and doing the recruiting itself. Allison was now working up to capacity, fully utilizing his strengths and talents, and connected passionately to the mission and vision of his employer. Most importantly, Allison was paying it forward every minute of every day.

When we first met, I had been hired to find an executive assistant for Allison, someone to help with his ever-increasing responsibilities at KIPP. I asked Allison if he thought he would ever go back to sales, fully expecting to hear that wasn't possible now that he had realized that his passion is working in nonprofit and paying it forward to the kids he serves through KIPP. Much to my surprise, Allison looked me right in the eye and said, "Maybe! I don't want to be perceived as perfect in any way. I don't have it all 'under control' by any means. If I worked in sales again, I could write bigger checks." We talked some about that, and Allison said, "Back in my days at the University of Pennsylvania, I met David Pottruck, former co-CEO of Schwab. David changed my life by talking with me. Maybe if there were a way I could reach people by writing bigger checks, I could impact more lives. The important thing I've learned is that I will never stop 'paying it forward' because that is where my passion lives. I've learned that I am just plain happier when I am living my passion of helping others. How exactly I do that is not important; that I do it is all-important. A key lesson I've learned is that you are happy because, somewhere in your life, you are living your passion."

From my perspective, I could imagine that the way Allison demonstrates that passion will change—and I suspected that the intensity of his commitment would not diminish. Over time, I learned that in the years since we first met, he had been doing contract fund raising for KIPP even while living in Africa, where his wife Dana, a pediatrician, was pursuing work with the Baylor International Pediatric AIDS Initiative (BIPAI), helping to build a pediatric AIDS clinic at Bobo-Dioulasso in Burkina Faso. He then took a job as the acting Southern Africa regional director for Room to Read, an organization whose focus is on developing literacy skills and the habit of reading in children of developing countries. In both capacities, he was using his skills in alignment with his passions and principles. During his stay in Africa, Allison found a variety of ways to pay it forward to a community halfway across the world from the community in which he had been reared.

When I met with Allison in 2011, I again asked if he would ever go back to sales, for the money. This time, he didn't qualify his answer, but simply said, "Never!" He and a colleague had recently founded EdVillage, with the goal of global partnership solutions to improve education in economically disadvantaged communities. With lessons and learnings gleaned from U.S.-based and international organizations (including alliances among the KIPP Foundation, Room to Read, and Teach For All), EdVillage is preparing future leaders to open the highest quality schools and create networks of schools where they are most needed. Allison's experience continues to be a perfect example of the fact that, when in right work—for Allison, work that aligns with his passion of paying it forward—the well never runs dry. Instead, those in right work are renewed and recharged by the work itself as they fulfill their purpose and contribute their gifts to the world.

I consider one of the major blessings of my life's work to be the fact that I have been fortunate to meet such a wide variety of people, from so many different industries and backgrounds. Many of my clients are very successful, perhaps in part because of their passionate commitment to giving as much of themselves as they possibly can to their work and to their communities. Like Allison, many of them have habits of paying it forward.

Years ago, as part of my practice of following my Grandma Edie's advice to pass it on, I attended a fundraiser for Women's Initiative for Self-Employment, an organization that supports low-income women in their entrepreneurial efforts. Before the dinner, guests visited the booths of program graduates who were offering their wares for sale. As I wandered around, I stopped and looked at a table that had hand-made bags and hand-crocheted bikinis for sale. A thoughtful-looking man stood next to me holding up one of the bikinis. "What do you think about me getting this for my wife?" he asked. I looked at him and thought he looked vaguely familiar, but no names came to mind. "Oh no," I laughed, "Never ever buy a woman a bikini if she hasn't tried it on. That is a dangerous move on lots of levels." He chuckled, thought for a moment, and said, "I think I'm going to buy it anyway and take my chances!"

Later, as I sat down at my assigned table, I was delighted to see that the risk-taking, bikini-buying man was seated next to me. "Well, hello!" I said, "I love that you went ahead and bought the bikini." I held out my hand and introduced myself.

"I'm Warren Hellman," he replied. Warren Hellman? No wonder his face had seemed familiar. We hadn't met before that day, but I'd seen his photos and knew a fair bit about him. In fact, my former company had placed executive assistants with Warren's international private equity firm's San Francisco office. His was one of the top private equity investment firms in the world, with offices in New York, London, and San Francisco. And here he was sitting right next to me. Not only that, but two extra people had been assigned to our table and we were sitting very close; as Warren said, with a gleam in his eye, we were "almost cheek to cheek."

Warren was in his early seventies and had the appearance and energy of a man twenty-five years younger: he laughed easily, was comfortable in his own skin, and clearly having great fun in his life. In between courses, I told him about my book, explaining that I wanted to tell the stories of people who had created work and lives they passionately loved. I said that I believed that when people were working and living in ways that used their unique talents and gifts, they experienced significantly greater success, happiness, and fulfillment than those whose work wasn't a good personal fit. Warren agreed both with my idea and to meet with me. We set a meeting for the following week.

Seconds after the receptionist announced my arrival, Warren came sprinting toward me with outstretched hand, to welcome me to his company and usher me into his office. The room was filled with memorabilia and stacked high with CDs, papers, and positively exuded the warmth and flair of Warren's personality. I saw no similarity whatsoever to any office of any investment banker or financial executive with whom I had met before. The office was absolutely one of a kind as was its occupant!

The two of us had initially met only days before, yet it felt as though I was visiting with someone I had known for a long time. Warren and I laughed about our meeting and our "cheek to cheek" evening. Instantly, we were deep in dialogue and I could sense that I was about to again be inspired by the story and the spirit of one human being's journey to creating a life he passionately loved.

By then I had done my homework and knew that Hellman was still active in his business, an effective contributor to the political well being and educational system of San Francisco, and a major philanthropist in ways that few people knew. Here was an authentic and gracious man who could certainly afford to relax in luxury for the remainder of his life. Instead, he was not just dual tracking, he was multitracking, and giving back to the world at a level hard to even imagine. One—mind you one—of the ways he gave back was through his wildly successful Hardly Strictly Bluegrass Festival, which was attended by 600,000 people in 2011, its eleven-year anniversary. The festival draws famous country western and bluegrass musicians from all over the country, from the big names like Emmylou Harris and Earl Scruggs to up and coming performers whose CDs pour into Warren's office. Every year, the attendees are amazed at the talent, the venue (Golden Gate Park), the multiple stages, and the fact that it's all free! Few of them know that the annual event was created by, organized by, and completely paid for by one person: Warren Hellman.

When I told Warren that I had attended his festival and was continually awestruck by the generosity of his gift to the people of San Francisco, I also shared with him that I could see that those who attended, as well as the musicians who played, were all enriched because of the festival. I told him I was betting that he felt he got a whole lot more back than he gave. "Oh," he said, "It is the most selfish thing I've ever done! You have no idea how much I get back. You just have no idea." I did have an inkling of how much the festival must cost, both in time and money, so for him to call it a selfish act gave me a good sense of the man.

Warren told me about an interchange he once had with a young hitchhiker who, when hearing the classical music playing on his radio, asked if it was his favorite music. When Warren responded that bluegrass was actually his favorite, she immediately piped up, "Me too! Do you know there is a man in San Francisco who pays for the entire Hardly Strictly Bluegrass Festival every year?" When he told her he was that man, she gasped, thanked him and gave him a giant hug and kiss on the cheek. Warren grinned at me and said, "Me, being an ego-driven male, do you know how that made me feel?"

"Did you ever have that same feeling when you closed a deal?" I asked.

"Not in this lifetime," Warren laughed. "Actually, though, when I looked around and watched the whole scene at the very first festival,

I felt I had died and gone to heaven." He mused for a few seconds, undoubtedly picturing festivals from other years, and continued, "Do you know who I get to meet? I get to hang out with Emmylou Harris, Hazel Dickens, Allison Brown. And I get to play music with them!" I smiled, just imagining working hard to create, organize, produce—and pay for—an event that makes you feel uplifted to such a degree. I had no doubt that the sheer happiness that Warren derived from the event itself more than balanced out the work he put into it; in fact, I guessed that it renewed him every year. As I was about to ask if that was true, Warren answered my unframed question by saying that he doesn't believe one should do anything to get thanked. "I do it because it is really, really fun. Philanthropy is really fun. Certainly it's not fun that people are in need or suffering, but if I can make any difference in the school system or in people's lives, it feels good. And I get to know a whole additional group of people."

Throughout our time together (and even in reviewing the transcript of our conversation), I kept having to remind myself that Warren worked and lived in a highly conservative "in the box" world where profit was king. That background made the fact that he gave away uncounted hours of his time and money to the general public with his free festival even more unusual. When I asked more about this, how his life had expanded way beyond his successful business career, Warren laughed his easy, almost self-deprecating, laugh. "It's pure indulgence. I can't articulate it very well, but most of my experiences are based on lessons I learned growing up. For example, my father had a serious drinking problem so I don't drink. Also, I was at Lehman Brothers for eighteen years before starting my own firm, and as a young partner I watched as a bunch of really intelligent, effective people got old and wandered around the firm with irrelevancy; despite having tons of money, they really had nothing. I didn't want to end up like that, begging for attention, hoping to be still relevant. I decided that I wouldn't be that way. I say that as you go on in life, if you have the will and means, indulge in the things that you love. For me, that's standing in the meadow with a hundred thousand people, all of whom are happy and all of whom love music. Countless positive experiences emerge from that sharing."

Was there a connection between the integrity of Warren's core, the level of his contribution to the world and the joy with which he lived? I knew that he made it a practice to arise at 3:30 in the morning, run six miles up and down San Francisco hills, and then read the Torah for an hour before work. Was his life so full because he spent time in morning exercise, contemplation, and spiritual practice? Were the self-awareness and tenacity Warren had developed the secrets to his fulfillment as a human being?

"Honestly," Warren replied, "what's key is just believing that nobody is better than anybody else. The last time I thought I was important was when, as a young partner at Lehman Brothers, I tried to arrange for Pete Seeger to give me banjo lessons. Finally, I got through to his manager, who hadn't ever heard of Lehman Brothers and certainly wouldn't let me talk to Pete Seeger. I realized then that no one is more important than anyone else." Warren continued, "I'm actually very mediocre in my music. I'm only successful because I persevere, not because I have any great talent. I am a reasonable investor, though not great. I have been really fortunate and pretty good at choosing people; I think that is the talent that I have. I guess, if I have a hobby, it is sort of collecting people who are fascinating to me—and most people are."

In my opinion, what made Warren truly wealthy was not just his financial success, but his integrity and his focus on giving to others, both of which, as far as I can tell, he exhibited throughout his entire life. As early as his twenties, Warren had demonstrated the courage to work and live without the need for others' approval. A few examples: in a time when all businessmen—certainly all of those at Lehman Brothers—wore hats to the office, he refused; when drinking alcohol was considered a part of doing business, he chose to not drink alcohol on business lunches, after work—or at all. These may seem like small differences now; they weren't then. He took banjo lessons. Hellman and his band, The Wronglers, often played in the San Francisco Bay Area, and always at the Hardly Strictly Bluegrass Festival. He created the Hellman Fellows Program to assist young professors financially before they had earned tenure. The list goes on. The Hardly Strictly Bluegrass Festival may be the most widely known of his contributions—and still many didn't know that Warren was the force and the funding behind it. Warren's generosity of spirit and his contributions had sprung from a great love of people and music, deep humility, his authenticity, and his extraordinarily well-developed self-discipline and self-reliance. He exhibited power, passion, and joy in giving and in living. He received giant daily doses of joy and fulfillment because of his passion for people and the game of life. He loved to help. He loved to mentor. He loved to inspire. His life reflected who he really was, not who others thought he should be.

When I learned of Warren's death on December 18, 2011, I thought back to our time together, and remembered that, as we closed our interview, Warren's eyes were sparkling with light and happiness. I told him that his very way of being reminded me of a quote by His Holiness, the Dalai Lama, who was in turn quoting an ancient Indian Sage, Shantideva: "All suffering is caused by thinking of one's self; all happiness is caused by thinking of others." Warren loved the quote—and I wasn't at all surprised. He clearly had determined his values and priorities and lived by them through many, many decades.

In a similar way, my friend Deb Wetherby exudes an air of deep happiness. With Deb, as with Warren, laughter is never far from the surface. This is a woman for whom work is a joy and well aligned with her values and talents. Deb was not born into money, but to parents whose main mantra was: "If you don't do something about it, you lose your right to whine." Deb's parents instilled in their children the belief that it was each person's responsibility to create the life they loved. Nobody else was responsible.

Deb graduated from the University of Virginia with a double major in finance and accounting. She moved to California to work as an accountant for Price Waterhouse, secured her CPA designation, and then her MBA from the University of California at Berkeley. Deb's enthusiasm and natural talent rapidly propelled her forward. Soon, she became one of the dozen women out of 145 high-net-worth brokers working on Wall Street for a prestigious bank in their international practice. The work came easily to her—and yet, something didn't feel right. She began to feel that the straight commission basis of her work was often in conflict with the best interest of her clients. The firm was driven, quite naturally, by a focus on bottom-line performance.

With conscious reflection, Deb began to determine what she liked about the job and what she didn't. Deb had always loved numbers. Even as a little girl, she calculated foreign exchange rates when her family lived in Europe. As an adult, she loved the broad look at the markets. She cared deeply about her clients and loved taking care of them with long-term investment strategies. But she hated the firm's focus on short-term commissions and on just "making money." In analyzing her situation, she knew that if she were to leave her employer, she would be giving up a fast track career that offered great wealth and prestige. She also knew that if she kept going the way she had been, she "would wake up one morning as a fifty-year-old single woman with great wealth and many toys. And I knew I would have missed out on meaning at a deep level. I had what was supposed to be the ultimate Wall Street job and I was miserable. Just moving to another firm wasn't going to change how I felt. Even good days became bad days. Either I had to embrace 'making money' as a more important value in my head, or get out. So I decided, at the ripe old age of thirty, that I wanted more meaning and less prestige."

Deb had made her choice. She left the bank under good terms, was introduced to some potential job opportunities, and took a three-month sabbatical in San Francisco. There, she began again to search for work she loved, this time on the West Coast. She wound up taking a job with a prestigious investment firm, one she had been drawn to because of its focus on the markets and its fee-based way of doing business. What Deb didn't know was that the firm's practices were not in line with her most important values. It took Deb six months of settling in before she realized that once again, something was "terribly wrong." She blamed herself for months, trying hard to fix what was part of the cultural context of the firm itself. But she saw that management would spread gossip about employees to one another; they would go through people's drawers and divide and conquer any team connection so as to better control people. Having realized she was compromising her own values and priorities by staying at a firm where she was not aligned at a core level, Deb jumped off yet one more cliff, this time with the goal of building her own business.

Deb's internal voice of doubt was loud; Darrell Adams, then her husband, recognized this and became her biggest cheerleader. As she questioned her decision and worried about the challenges ahead, Darrell asked, time and again, "What is the worst that can happen?" Deb had many fears and anxieties about taking the huge leap to self-employment: the morass of regulatory requirements, concerns about administrative needs, fears of clients not showing up and of expenses mounting. The list continued. "I had so many fears. I questioned the information coming from my heart because it was 'illogical.' I second-guessed myself, wondering 'Is it right? Am I crazy?' I was the main breadwinner in our family. I had anxiety about money and a mortgage to pay. I knew that other people would have loved the job I'd quit. What was wrong with me? My biggest fear was that I would make mistakes and fail."

I asked Deb what she did when she was overcome with fear. Without a moment's hesitation, she said, "I was raised with the focus on moving into action. No complaints, no whining. When I get scared, I get moving. I made a list of all the things I had said I would do if I ever had the time. There were twenty-five or more things, like play the guitar and improve my French. When I was anxious, I would just start on my list. I still find that making lists diminishes anxiety tremendously."

After reviewing all of her experiences (in effect, writing her career autobiography), Deb realized that each and every one of her jobs had taught her more about who she really was, about her core values and her strongest abilities. In not much time, she was crystal clear about her vision for her new business. She was also clear that if she failed, she would simply do what she would have done if she hadn't taken the leap to start her own business: she would work for someone else. That was "the worst that could happen." With her backup plan tucked away, Deb put her fears neatly in her briefcase and hung out her own shingle. As she said to me, "Funny enough, when I look back on it, only 5 percent of my fears ever came to pass. Five percent! I did make mistakes. I own them. I apologize. I learn from them; now the entire firm learns from them. It's not a big deal and it's part of being human."

The entire firm? Wetherby Asset Management has thrived, from the solo practice Deb started in 1990 to a business with nearly fifty people, even in these difficult markets. Deb now owns one of the biggest advisory firms in the country, managing $3.6 billion in client assets. She is often quoted in the national media and passionately, unconditionally, loves what she does. Deb has been able to do well by following the values and principles she holds most dear, including working with clients who also hold the values of integrity, honesty, and care. And always, clients come first; commissions don't exist.

The rules and tips Deb passed on as we spoke can help anyone in search of right work.

- Pay attention to what gives you joy.
- Pay attention to what comes easily and what you do well.
- We always have choices, no matter what stage of life. Be clear about your choices and the prices you pay for them.
- Identify your values and what is important to you; never, ever compromise those values for any reason.

- Ask yourself: What is the worst that can happen if you fail? Once you see that the worst that can happen is what you would do anyway, there is much less fear.
- You don't have to perceive the total outcome; however, at every decision point you must be true to yourself.
- Remember that if you look back on your life and realize that you never tried something you'd hoped to, you will probably have big regrets. If you tried and failed, you probably will have no regret.

I thought it a safe bet that, given the success she has had, Deb has no regrets about her big leap. She smiled and said, "Each time I made a change in my career, I got more of what I loved and less of what didn't work for me. I never really knew if this was the ultimate job. But I knew that if I kept working on what I liked and what was right for me, and what I was good at, I would end up in the right place. Now I've definitely ended up in the right place." Deb is planning a year sabbatical in the years ahead. She plans to take time for self-reflection and philanthropy.

For Deb, discovering her own right work has been a continuing process, full of growth and change. And, in my experience, that's how it works, since everyone's needs and priorities change over time. The allegiance to underlying personal values, however, remains constant. Those who don't acknowledge and attend to those values wind up— as Deb had feared she might, and as Warren Hellman had sworn he wouldn't—suddenly at a dead end that means nothing to them and that doesn't seem relevant or of value to the world.

A consistent practice I've seen in those who have found their right work and are successful beyond their imaginings is that they periodically revisit the idea of what is right work for them: they make a conscious effort to ensure that as their work evolves it remains in line with their values, strongest talents, and their current priorities.

As you identify your own right work, be sure to recognize your present stage of life. In my experience, many of us develop habits of working (24/7 in early career stages, for example) that then become fixed in later years, continuing even long after that level of intensity has been necessary. We haven't realized that we no longer need to expend as much effort as we did at the beginning. Our habits haven't changed with our priorities and mastery of work. In my work now, with four decades of experience, I can sometimes send only one candidate who is a perfect fit for my client rather than many more. This leaves time to write a book or develop other interests and practices.

If, however, you're a recent college graduate with only a little experience in the work place and college loans coming due, one of your top priorities will be finding employment that pays as much as possible while you are paying off the loans. Whether or not you have loans that factor into your decisions, you have the benefit of knowing—in advance—that your first job is most likely the first of many and that your work will evolve over time. In a way, knowing that yours is not a once-in-a-lifetime decision can be liberating. Today's job market is far from the lockstep career world that earlier generations entered. Instead, just as your priorities and passions can (and likely will) change over time, job opportunities will change as well. Researchers tell us that we don't even know the names of 60 percent of the jobs that will be available in twenty years. Develop career self-reliance now as you identify your strengths, values and priorities, commit to lifelong learning, and learn now how to create work that is consistently right for you at each stage of your life.

If you're at a later stage in life and you look back carefully at times when you may have felt stuck in work, or that you knew you were in wrong work, it is likely that your gifts were not being used, or your priorities and values were not being supported in that work. If you are currently in work that you no longer enjoy, there is a good chance that your priorities have shifted and your work no longer supports those revised priorities. All the more reason to have regular times in which you assess where you are, where you'd like to go (figuratively and liter-ally), and what you need to do differently. And all the more reason to prepare a career autobiography and keep it current. As you'll see in the Action Items later in the book, this doesn't mean writing a full-blown autobiography, but rather spending time noting what you have liked and done well over the years relative to work (along with a raft of other personal information). At this point, it's for your eyes only, to help you see what bubbles up, what interests you've developed, what lessons you've learned (and are learning) from what you like and don't like (or like less).

Whatever your stage, I believe that the most important two ques-tions you can ask yourself in defining your own right work are these:

- At this stage in my life, what are my top priorities relative to work?
- At this point in time, what do I know to be my strongest tal-ents, skills, and abilities?

These are not simple questions, but questions to ponder after you have done the self-reflection and information gathering described later in this book. As you address these questions, be inclusive as you list your priorities, talents, skills, and abilities; then rank them in order of their importance to you.

Knowing this, and having advised people to regularly reevaluate their right work, I should not have been surprised one evening when Linda Wosskow quietly announced to me that she was looking into sell-ing her company, Oyé Productions, and wanted me to begin to search for a full-time job for her. It was Linda who, years previous, had used the magic wand (and dual tracking) to realize her dream of developing a business in brokering Latin musicians. (Her story is in chapter 2.)

"Why?" I asked. "You are my poster child for finding right work! Why would you want to leave what you love so much?" Linda looked at me with much gentleness in her eyes and replied, "I have loved my business! I have loved watching the smiles of musicians I placed in gigs. Everyone smiled; we've all had the best time. I am so happy to have done it all these years. I cannot tell you how happy I am that I did it! But my priorities have changed again. I've just turned sixty. Now, what is becoming more important to me is that I have a stable, steady income and some benefits. So," she smiled, "Can you help me?"

Linda did sell her company and tucked the money and residuals away into her retirement fund. I placed her as the executive assistant to the CEO of a nonprofit organization in San Francisco whose purpose it is to inspire business leaders to work together on civic issues. The organization works on transportation, education, housing, jobs and anything that impacts the economic and quality of life of the entire San Francisco Bay Area. There, Linda used her talent for networking and proactively supporting projects and people in a new arena: instead of musicians, she coordinated the activities of her CEO and the CEO members of the organization.

Linda's core talents, passions, and love of service had stayed the same. But at age sixty, her priorities had shifted. Looking to retirement, the benefits and stable paycheck, along with the opportunity to increase her Social Security contribution bumped up on her list. Still later in her life, when she wanted to work closer to her home (another natural shift in priorities), she chose to work with a nonprofit that helps the homeless.

Recently, I asked Linda if she was sorry she had sold her business. I knew that the Internet, which had been a boon to Linda's business in its beginning stages, had become a competitor of sorts once Google arrived on the scene. People could search musicians they found on Linda's website and hire them directly without needing to call Linda and pay her fee. "Absolutely not! When I sold the company, I was finished with the business. Things had changed and my priorities were different than they had been. What was so wonderful and what has made me so happy is that I realized a dream I had held all of my life without even knowing it. Had I stayed in my old job, I'm sure I would have gotten sick. Instead, in founding Oyé Productions, I not only found new work, I found a dream come true. Do you know how good that feels?"

Dual tracking had worked for Linda. And, as I learned, it had worked for her in a slightly different sense even in her childhood and then in her first job. As far back as she could remember, Linda had loved music and dancing. As a child in England, she would sneak the radio into her room late at night and listen to Radio Luxembourg. At age thirteen or fourteen, she would slip out to a blues club and listen to the old black blues singers, John Lee Hooker, Jimmy Witherspoon, and T-Bone Walker. She was not, as her parents thought, visiting a friend— but she knew that with music or dance, her soul soared.

Once I knew this about Linda, I was not surprised to learn that after graduating from secretarial college, her very first job was in London's West End, known as Britain's Tin Pan Alley because it's where all the music companies were then headquartered in London. Linda would go to sleep right after work, get up at midnight, and dance in the clubs until morning. Then, she would go to work, come home, and repeat the drill, daily. It sounds exhausting—unless it's what you love. And it fits the pattern I've seen in people who are in work they love: their energy is constantly renewed, such that it seems boundless. That, in a nutshell, is the joy of work you love. Getting paid to do what you love fills you up and restores your energy. Loving what you get paid to do does the same. As long as your work is aligned with your top life priorities, utilizes your strongest talents and gifts, and supports your values, you will love what you do.

The steps included in the third set of Action Items at the end of the book, "Identify and Find Your Right Work" (outer and inner together), provide more detailed guidance to help ensure that you make a thorough evaluation of yourself as you determine your own right work. To get the most from this process, you will need to draw on what you've learned in addressing the first two sets of Action Items—"Prepare to Be Prepared" (outer) and "Take Time for Reflection" (inner).

In my search business, we often assign potential candidates the task of writing a brief work or career autobiography. It helps them clarify their goals and provides a useful entry point for me to assess the likelihood of a strong match with the needs of one of our clients. Here are the directions we provide.

> Describe the jobs you have held in your professional career for the past five to fifteen years. In your description, please include the following:
> — The priorities that led you to take each job and the reasons for remaining with the job.
> — Your primary responsibilities.
> — The biggest challenge you overcame.
> — Your biggest contribution and each job's biggest contribution to you.
> — The aspect of each job you most enjoyed.
> — The aspect of each job or that was unappealing or difficult.
> — Why you left your previous jobs.
>
> Be sure to address four more general questions:
> — What are your top five priorities relative to your current search for work?
> — If we talked to people who know you best, what would all of them be likely to remember most about you relative to work?
> — What do you believe is your strongest talent or gift that you bring to your work?
> — What do you consider to be your biggest contribution relative to work?
>
> Please limit your response to a maximum of three pages, double spaced.

This short form serves its purpose very well. Candidates take some time for introspection and come to me with a window into what they've done and what they're looking for.

chapter 5

Trust Your Inner Wisdom

It is wisdom to believe the heart.

GEORGE SANTAYANA, SPANISH PHILOSOPHER AND ESSAYIST

Having read the previous chapters and learned about four of the steps to discovering your right work—jump, let go (of needing to know), assess your talents and skills, identify your priorities and values—and perhaps even begun some of the related Action Items, now comes the step that is the catalyst for discovery of your right work. Acknowledging and tapping into your inner wisdom is the access road to the powerful insights and strength that support your process in moving through all the steps with confidence and faith that the answers are there. You've seen that inner wisdom in action in this book's stories, read of how that inner wisdom has guided people into work that does more than simply sustain them, how it enriches them so that the wells of energy and resources never run dry. You've seen how it guides them into creating work that expands their lives as individuals and as part of their immediate community—and their contributions to the larger world. If you've looked ahead to the Action Items, you've seen that there's more to the process than reading about right work and imagining it. There are specific tasks and practices to undertake and to learn. Since you've read this far, they're all easier . . . and still, there are cliffs ahead. But you're not alone: we all face a variety of cliffs throughout our lives.

Over the years, I've known more than a few people who have jumped off multiple cliffs—and who have landed with extraordinary grace. This chapter on inner wisdom seems the appropriate chapter to tell the story of one in particular, a close friend and confidant I met long before I began this book, even before I began thinking of it.

It was 1990 and I was in Reno, Nevada attending a conference on "Growing Your Business," co-sponsored by *Inc.* magazine and Porsche. At the time, my mindset was that when it came to my company, bigger was definitely better. I owned a large staffing agency in San Francisco and was on a fast track to expand the business still further. The truth is that expanding my business was not the only reason I had signed up. The other reason I was there? Attendees would have the opportunity to test drive a high-performance Porsche on a real racetrack. That perk certainly wasn't offered at any of the other conferences I had considered.

When I crawled behind the wheel of the Porsche I was to drive, I had the same high excitement as when I had climbed into the cockpit of the F4 fighter jet my USN former husband flew out of San Diego—with one big difference. I wasn't going to take the F4 for a ride and I was going to take the Porsche! In the little cockpit of that Porsche, my feelings of big power, speed, and anticipation were surrounded by abject terror. I had noticed that there were only a few women at the conference; there were even fewer of us at the racetrack. Interestingly enough, the men had eagerly jockeyed for positions in line; they couldn't wait. I, however, was uncharacteristically timid. Gender equality aside, this was an epiphany for me: I had no doubt that testosterone was a vastly different fuel than estrogen.

We had been instructed how to take the car from standing to 120 miles per hour. I was buckled in tightly. The door was closed. It was me, my estrogen, and the racetrack ahead. I took a very deep breath before placing my foot on the accelerator. Down went my foot. Whoosh! Up, up, up, went the speedometer. The Porsche flew as though we were above the ground. Round the track we went, taking the turns like a pro and, suddenly, I felt that my fear had been left far, far behind. After my allotted number of laps, I slowed the car down and stopped in front of my clapping colleagues. I felt so good I thought I would burst.

As the years rolled on after that memorable moment, I often thought back about those trips around the racetrack—especially when I was afraid to jump off the next very high cliff. There were certainly lessons for me in that ride, as there were lessons and gifts in the rest of the conference.

One of the sessions I chose to attend was on the subject of increasing client loyalty through relationship building. The speaker began by telling us that he had just run across the United States in support of a nonprofit he had helped start, a nonprofit whose focus was on a "Drug-Free California." I knew right away that I was in for an interesting presentation. Little did I know that I was about to begin a lifelong friendship with someone whose work has inspired me, and many, many others to go within and lead from the heart. Naturally that speaker, Terry Pearce, was one of the first people I thought to interview when I began my book about finding right work, many years after we first met. Terry's story could well illustrate each of the steps and could certainly fill a book on its own; to my mind, this chapter on inner wisdom is truly where it belongs.

Terry had grown up in Oregon and lived for a time on a small farm where morning chores came early and expectations for fun and fulfilling futures were few. His mother died when Terry was a young teen. His father was a railroad conductor for many years and Terry worked summers pounding nails into railroad ties to earn spending money. No one in Terry's family had ever graduated from college; his dreams were different than all of his family and most of his friends. Even as a child, Terry knew in secret that he marched to a different drummer. What he didn't know was where that drummer would lead him.

Terry's intellect and his charismatic presence were a signature part of the many variations in his successful career. Yet he admitted to having been painfully shy, which seemed in such contrast to his powerful public presence. I asked how he had gotten from the boy in rural Oregon to where he was today, consulting and inspiring people on an international level. As one step, he had financed his dream of going to college by playing music in a band, working in construction, and cobbling together scholarships and a small loan from a devoted grandmother.

Was there something Terry learned in his early years of poverty and adversity that formed his secret steps to discovering work he loved—and that ultimately paved the path to his own success and happiness? Terry is a great example of someone in completely right work, someone who has consistently been able to reinvent himself in ever more powerful ways of contributing to the world. He uses his talents and gifts, contributes to the world, and loves what he does. He's had three or four different careers, different eras of work, each one with more depth and impact than the one before.

When Terry was in his early sixties, he began anew yet again, enrolling in a graduate program in comparative mythology, with an emphasis in depth psychology, at the Pacifica Graduate Institute in Santa Barbara, California. A few years into his studies, with deep concerns about the dire environmental, political, and economic straits the world is facing, Terry brought thought leaders from around the world together to explore the roots of inspiration, and what might inspire global progress. He's tackling big issues—and all while consulting with leaders internationally through his consulting practice, Leadership Communication.

I wanted to know how he got there. Who had mentored young Terry? How had he known his direction and where had he found his answers? What steps had he taken to find or create work he loved, work that was such a perfect match for his talents? And another big one: How did he overcome the core beliefs into which he was born: that one got a job, worked hard to keep it, felt lucky to get a paycheck and feed the family, and then retired and died? "Let's go back to the farm," I said to Terry. "Let's talk about the little boy and his dreams and how it all happened. Let's look at all the times you reinvented yourself so successfully. What steps did you take? What are your 'secrets'?"

Terry sat back, smiled at me, and responded: "When you said, just 'go back to the farm,' you are exactly right. Now, in retrospect, I can see how my life has been an unfolding rather than a series of reinventions. But when you're in it, you can't see that—or I couldn't. I've tried to get my children to understand this, to understand that core, this uniqueness to their lives that they're born to roll out. And if they're able or willing to discover that early in life they'll have a much longer, happier link to times when they're actually enjoying and living life in the way that they are meant to be living it. I wish I had seen it so much earlier; I wouldn't have resisted so much. I've tried to tell my children this, for the younger you are when you understand it, the more valuable it will be."

I asked Terry to tell me what he's learned about his unfolding life. Does he just jump off cliff after cliff and hope he won't land in a heap at the bottom? How does he know when he's working according to the best possible plan for him—and for the world?

Terry laughed. "When I'm asked questions like yours, my ego wants to tell everyone that every step of the way happened on purpose. My ego would love to just take credit for everything. But when I was living it, I often had no idea what I was doing. If there's been something true about it, it's been that I've been able to hear and been willing to follow a voice inside of me and I've had the courage—or had been panicked enough—to follow that voice and to move in that direction when it calls."

I know how hard it is for some people to hear their inner voice. Many don't even know it's there; those who do recognize it may not fully trust it. So I asked Terry, "How is it that you made time to 'go within' amid such a full life? What made you able to follow that voice?

Did someone encourage you or did you just know? In our culture, people don't generally go around talking about hearing voices and following them, right?"

Terry's response was instant: "Right! I would love to say that I had some kind of enlightened sense, but I didn't. I do believe, in retrospect, that the voice was so strong in me that not following it would have had penalties. So that's one thing: life becomes what I would consider to be unbearable if I don't listen. The other thing is that when you start to follow that voice, good things happen. That is when the universe creates magic and synchronicity comes into play. For almost a century, depth psychologists have been telling us that synchronicity actually is, for lack of a better word, the response of God or the response of the Spirit to your affirmation of it. So when you follow this voice, positive things come into your path: you start to meet the right people, you grow as you need to, you find the right job, new resources show up. Why don't most people do it? Because we don't recognize the voice. I mean it's as though, when Moses saw the burning bush and heard the voice of God saying, 'This is Yahweh' Moses critiqued it, saying (or thinking), 'How do I know this is Yahweh? How do I know it's not some mugger?'"

I thought about Terry's words and my own life. My Quaker upbringing had taught me to sit in the silence and "mind the light of God within." What was the "light"? It was a kind of voice, wasn't it? It was the nudge towards or away from one thing or another, one person or another, one place or another, one job or another. Hadn't my own light been directed from within? Hadn't my own "voices" been stronger and stronger the older I got and the more I listened? This conversation certainly resonated; I asked Terry to continue.

As Terry explained, "What makes hearing your own voice difficult is that the voice of your parents is so strong. And the voice of other people around you telling you what's good and what's bad is so loud. You learn to trust your voice by jumping off and having faith in that feeling that you have inside of you and then getting the affirmation back from the rest of the world. Or at least, that is the only way I've discovered to be sure. Certainly action is necessary. You have to listen, hear the voice, and take the chance. If you're following the right voice, then resources start to come to you and then you start to live out of that place, with increasing confidence in your voice, your inner wisdom."

Thanks to my Grandma Edie and my early Quaker upbringing, I too had listened to the voice within. I had followed that voice when I moved back to California as a young divorced single mother. I had followed that voice when I took my first job in an employment agency working on straight commission and again with each reinvention of my own career. And now, I am following that voice as I write this book. I know that Terry is right: each time you listen to the voice, it gets easier to hear. And when you heed that voice, life becomes easier, more meaningful, and more on track for you. But I know that finding the time to shut off the world long enough to hear anything other than the noise of modern life—to go within—can be hard. I knew that Terry had run across the country and that he had jogged fifty miles on his fiftieth birthday. Maybe he used his time jogging to listen to his inner voice?

Terry heard my questions and picked right up, saying, "It's true: the more time you're alone, the more opportunity you have to hear the voice. And the more you can shut your regular mind off by giving it some practice, time in which it has an opportunity to get through the clutter and actually hear something other than the voice of the world, the more possibility you have to hear it. As a child, I learned a way of being by myself, a kind of self-reliance, probably out of pure desperation; I learned I could be alone in an imaginative reality."

"Aha!" I said, "You looked to yourself for answers and support rather than parents and teachers. As a child, you learned that you had resources separate from the outside world. So this ability to access inner wisdom—to hear the voice, to be guided into your life's purpose, your life's work—began back when you were little, perhaps when it seemed that your parents did not understand some of the things you were dreaming about. The voice you identified guided you; the more it took you places that were fulfilling, the more you listened. So, for you, being guided from within and living with self-reliance started long ago, on the little farm in Oregon!"

"Right." Terry said. "And I didn't realize that until I was fifty years old." We looked at each other, knowing we were both well over fifty years old, and laughed. We knew our children seemed to be more aware of things in their thirties than we had been, and that in some ways we were more aware in our thirties than our parents had been. So that was a good thing. But how wonderful if what we knew could be passed on so that the next generations didn't have to wait until they were thirty, forty, or fifty to be fully engaged in their life's purpose.

As Terry continued to tell his story, he spoke about his first real job after college—as a salesman with IBM in the sixties. In today's terms, that would be akin to landing a job with Google. The money was good: Terry's starting salary was the same amount of money his dad was making, after twenty-five years with the railroad. Terry rose quickly through the ranks, was sent to headquarters in New York, and was soon managing a forty million dollar business for IBM. Chosen for senior management, he had been tapped for the highest ranks of success. And yet the culture began to feel stifling; the demands on his time and the impact on his family felt excessive. Terry began to experience depression; later, he began to feel physically ill. At the time, he wondered if he lacked the courage for the next step. Terry declined a promotion and instead accepted a lateral move with IBM, telling himself that a major reason was so the family could be near his wife's parents in California. Deep down, he knew better. In retrospect, Terry saw that the voice had been leading him away, far away from IBM. Slowly, his voice was making itself known again. As Terry said, "That part of my life was coming to an end. It was the beginning of a very large transition; oddly, at about thirty-two or thirty-three years old, I was coming to the end of that very long cycle."

Did he remember the moment he knew he was going to leave IBM? Sure enough, he did: "I was in New York, espousing certain changes to the company and to my particular division. And I realized that my thinking was far different from that of my superiors in the company. I realized that I had moved to a place where I had perhaps an idealistic notion of what the company could be and become—and that other people thought I was crazy. My senior officers told me that my ideas would be totally out of line and not in keeping with IBM's corporate philosophy. At that point I knew I was going to leave. We essentially came to a mutually satisfactory separation agreement and I left—not knowing at all what my next step was going to be. That was concurrent with my divorce, concurrent with my getting full custody of my two boys. Life was going to be a totally different adventure. It was a major, major change."

How had he found the courage to leave the status and security of IBM? Terry explained that he had clearly felt pulled rather than pushed and, as he became aware of a voice inside, he paid more attention to his discomfort with IBM. As he said, "The core for me, the secret, was to know when it was over and to be able to hear the voice that was quite loud in me. It visited me with suggestions, then incantations, and then demands. And that arrived in the form of some kind of psychic upset; the force was definitely there, moving in me." As he told me, each time he began a new phase of his career, he knew, at a deep level, that the price for not following his path would have been that of living "a life of quiet desperation," a life that often results in illness and even early death.

He had experienced a meteoric rise to success at IBM; had he ever regretted leaving the company? Did he ever think he made the biggest mistake of his life? He told me that even in the hardest times, he hadn't wanted to return to IBM, but that "there were plenty of times when I thought I should have taken another job, one of the opportunities with other companies. And there were times when I questioned my own wisdom and even my own sanity in not accepting one of those positions. With regard to the family, there were many nights when I would cry myself to sleep, thinking that I had made a disastrous mistake. And yet my world was opening so rapidly that I couldn't deny that there was some force at work that I had to follow, that I had to answer. I was learning so much in California. I was growing and changing. I could no longer go back to the corporate world in New York."

I was reminded of my own life, of the many nights I had cried myself to sleep. My decision to move back to California after a divorce at the age of twenty-three had meant leaving a large extended support structure back East and it meant I would be raising my daughter alone. I had come back to San Francisco with a toddler, $300 in my pocket, no place to live, and no job. I had received a degree in eighteenth-century German literature and had no idea what people would pay me to do. And yet, I had been guided to San Francisco—and then to the Richmond District of the city. I was standing the sidewalk when a man tapped me on the shoulder and gently asked if I was looking for an apartment. "Yes," I said, "but I have a child and no job yet." "No worries," he had replied, "I can tell you will work hard." Paul Sing, my future landlord, didn't seem to mind that I didn't have a security deposit. The apartment was all that I could have wished for, and more: it was around the corner from a grocery store, it was right on the bus line that went to a preschool and on to downtown, it had brand new appliances, and it was fully carpeted. All of this mattered a great deal, since my daughter was two years old and I had no car. Especially amazing were the carpets, because until we could afford a bed, we had to sleep on them.

I felt blessed that my inner voice had spoken to me that day and guided me to the spot on Twelfth Avenue where I met Paul Sing. Was it just luck? Or was I learning to listen?

I thought more about "the voice." In my darkest moments, had I ever thought I shouldn't have listened to its guidance? Never. But until my conversation with Terry, I had never taken inventory as to how many times the voice had guided me to important next jobs or homes or people or books or ideas. I wondered if Terry had ever not listened to his voice? Did he always have faith in it?

Turns out, when Terry didn't listen to his voice, he got reminders to do so. Some were physical, some were from his studies and readings. As he put it, "I got progressively introduced to broader and broader concepts of what existence was and what my life would be." Terry was always a seeker of new ideas and psychological and spiritual truth. And, as the years went by, he started to have some small intuitive experiences of spiritual illumination, what the Zen Buddhists refer to as *satori*, and "some experiences of the world as something that I hadn't perceived it to be." He began to see that "there was much more unity and much more interconnectedness" in the world than he had previously realized. "By then, I had a pretty healthy meditation practice and I was looking at the world through those eyes."

I, too, had learned to meditate and quickly noticed that my days were easier and happier when I meditated than when I didn't. Was there a cause and effect relationship? Did one's ability to hear the voice increase when there was time for reflection, time to go within, time to stop the loud chatter of modern life?

Terry is a strong advocate for listening to the voice. For, "even if you fall, that fall is part of the process and part of the learning you'll need to move ahead. Certainly I've not always made the best decision. But the reason I'm making the decision is that I'm turning in the right direction. In time, I'll be guided to where I need to be. Someone or something will tell me, 'Hey, you took the wrong turn there.' Usually it's a pretty clear signal. Sometimes it's grace, sometimes it's a slap. The slaps get more severe as I get older. The need to pay attention gets more serious." I knew that Terry felt strongly that there was a synchronicity about life that supported him; when he is on the path—when any of us is on the right path—people and resources show up.

I also knew that sometime after Terry had left IBM and begun to rear his two boys alone, after his wife and daughter had left in the divorce—and at a time when the world was locked in the deep freeze of a Cold War and the potential of a nuclear winter—he had taken on a very serious task. Through his readings and practices (including study of *A Course in Miracles*), he had developed a sense of the power of the individual and of "the moral imperative to act on the knowledge that's coming in." It was then, right after Reagan was elected president, that "through synchronicity" he met a person of like mind, a man who was also very concerned about the world political situation, and the prevailing attitudes toward the nuclear question. As Terry told me, "the nuclear issue was number one on both of our lists. And, after some experience and some conversation, the two of us arrogantly decided that we might actually have an impact on the world political situation." It was 1982 and, as Terry put it, "a philosophy of mutually-shared destruction was seen to be in place and inevitable in terms of our foreign policy. And it was seen that way by a number of different cultures. We were hoping for a different level of possibility and started to explore ways in which we could influence leadership around the world. We focused particularly on three leaders—leaders of the Soviet Union, the United States, and the People's Republic of China—to find a way not necessarily to end armament but to declare that as a possibility. And in doing so, to start or to give the impetus to the rearranging of the facts so they would actually become reality."

I had to interject, and asked, "Is it safe to say that people thought you two might be a little cuckoo taking on this task?"

Terry flashed a smile. "That," he said, "would go down as one of the largest understatements of the year." They were laughed at by colleagues, family, and friends. Even so, they went to Stanford Research Institute in 1983 and suggested that the Institute sponsor a multiclient study in which they would ask this question: "What would be the result in terms of resource allocation and what would be the implications for the major corporations of the world if there was a nuclear disarmament accord between the East and the West, and the Berlin Wall were to come down both physically and metaphorically by 1988?" With a bit of a gleam in his eye, Terry explained that the Institute's then-president told them, in no uncertain terms, that "we were absolutely crazy and that he would either have to do that study as a one-page editorial in the newspaper or he would have to bet the Institute. That said, he summarily dismissed us from his office."

But they worked at it for years, made their connections, contacted Heads of State. I can reveal no more of this remarkable story, except to wonder: if these two men hadn't listened and acted, hadn't undertaken what they called the Initiative, would Reagan and Gorbachev have signed the Intermediate-Range Nuclear Forces (INF) Treaty in 1987? Might the Berlin Wall have stood much longer than the fall of 1989? Hard to know, but what is clear is that the idea of opening the possibility had spoken to Terry and his colleague in a way that they could not ignore: they listened and acted.

In parallel with their multiyear efforts, Terry knew he was going to have to go back and make a living. With his net worth greatly diminished and his two boys growing fast and getting about ready to go to college, he started to look for ways to use what he'd learned through the Initiative and through his earlier work with IBM in order "to replenish the piggy bank." Terry said, "There were some principles around communication and leadership that I was able to tease out and that became the launch of my next enterprise, which started in a little office in San Rafael. I had a small computer and a few ideas that I grew into Leadership Communication, my current company. Some would say that this was the kind of idea that had no chance of succeeding and that I certainly had no chance of making it successful. And yet people appeared and circumstances arranged themselves so that I had an opportunity to build a body of knowledge. I had clients who showed up and sponsored this work with their own executives. I was fairly successful in times when business logic would say it couldn't be."

Terry continued, saying, "I was speaking to a group at Berkeley by invitation when the Dean of the Haas School of Business happened to wander in; he then asked me if I wanted to teach a course at the university. Later, as I was thinking about documenting the principles in communication and writing a book about it, all of the resources that I needed showed up. The jobs and opportunities that opened up for me were quite remarkable; I've never wanted for anything. Everything—from clients to housing—seemed to fall in place once I had that core idea that this—Leadership Communication—was my right work and it was what I was supposed to do."

I knew Terry was understating his accomplishments, that he teaches internationally and that his book, *Leading Out Loud*, is used across the world. I looked at him and asked, "But what about while you were in the midst of starting? How did you manage the fear of not knowing? People are programmed to think that following the Golden Rule, money in the bank, 2.5 children well raised, and a boat in the backyard is a life well lived. How is it that you were able to deepen your contribution so much more? How were you able to move again and again into the unknown? Did you know where you would end up? What did you know when you began in a new direction, say with the Initiative? Or with starting your own business? Or with Charles Schwab & Company? Or more recently, when you went back to graduate school? And then when you developed the Forum on Cross-Cultural Inspiration?"

"What did I know?" Terry responded, "I know you can't control how it turns out. You can know the direction, but you can't control how it turns out. With the Initiative, we took on something so big, such a big vision, that acting alone, we could not possibly have arranged the meetings that we needed. When one door was closed to us, we knew that another one would open because that's what we were supposed to be doing." Often they found themselves following along the path they had set and suddenly came to a huge impasse. As Terry put it, "when we'd come to a brick wall, it was as though we'd feel along the wall for the loose brick, for the possible way in. Eventually we would discover it—often it would be revealed to us." Bringing it forward a few years, Terry said, "Going back to school was a door opening. It has expanded my perception, my perspective by a multiple of five or ten. I have quadruple the tools that I had before I started my studies at Pacifica. I have an understanding of depth psychology. I can now explain in scientific and psychological terms much of what my life has been about. And that has brought wealth for me going forward to be able to have an appeal to a group of people who would demand scholarly explanation or more objective reasons for moving in the direction that I want to try to get to." Terry saw my quizzical expression, and continued: "I see the world's biggest issue right now as the fundamental differences in the belief systems that we have and our failure to be able to tap something that will inspire us all, regardless of the base stories or mythologies of our belief systems. We need an ability to inspire people regardless of what their fundamental myths are. So that's what I'm learning and that's where I'll be moving with this next part of my life. Exactly how that will take shape, I don't know."

The fact that Terry appeared utterly relaxed and confident about this next stage of his life was not lost on me. He had years and careers of experience with change and knew, without a doubt, that he was on the right path for his gifts and his goals in life. I knew we would continue this conversation and delve more deeply into the topics in the years to come.

Perhaps because my conversation with Terry had me more alert to sources of inspiration, I soon happened upon a newspaper article titled "A Site of Inspiration." My eyes were drawn to the picture of a young man peering out through a stand of bamboo and to the caption that gave his name as Rhett Butler. Really? Could that actually be his given name or was it an alias, a way to draw attention—at least from the fans of *Gone with the Wind*? As I read the article, I saw that whatever his real name, in contrast to the often quoted line from the movie version of Margaret Mitchell's novel ("Frankly, my dear, I don't give a damn!"), this Rhett Butler did indeed "give a damn."

In fact, he gave a damn about vast global issues that, for most of us, seem too big to even think about. I visited his website, Mongabay. com, and was immediately drawn into content, stories, and magnificent photography from around the world. He had taken on huge environmental issues without raising his voice one bit. The site felt like my favorite kind of vacation: a journey to exotic places with a high level of learning and education. In addition, this was a site built from a place of passion and creativity and it was credible, thoroughly researched, and accurate. It truly was a site of inspiration.

Was Rhett Butler really making a living doing this work? And if so, how did he get to the place of being able to do that? He was so young, I wondered how he had known what he wanted to do. Had this been a passion of his as a child? The article mentioned that he had grown up in Atherton, California, which I knew as a very wealthy community where many of my CEO clients live. Was Rhett's story that of a rich young man being supported by doting parents? If not, if he had managed to find work he loved all by himself, what steps had he taken to get there? What was it that made him so different from the underprepared, slightly dazed college graduates I often saw in my recruiting business? If he was so driven, why had he not been drawn into the vortex of an exciting startup in his home turf of Silicon Valley as so many of his contemporaries had?

When I called Rhett, I was struck by the calmness in his voice and manner. There was no sense of being in a hurry, no frenetic energy. I was thrilled that Rhett agreed to make time to meet with me. In preparing for our interview, I had reviewed Rhett's websites and had seen the final paragraph of the preface to his second book, *A Place Out of Time*, which offered encouragement about the future: "A lot can still be done. Using our intelligence and ingenuity, the human species can preserve biodiversity and unique places for future generations, without compromising the quality of life for present populations."

Rhett was the youngest person I had yet interviewed for the book, but from everything I had learned, he was wise beyond his years. I found myself already filled with respect and admiration, even before meeting him. When we met, I quickly saw that Rhett has a quiet, strong presence and exudes competency and courage. He also has a sweet humility about him and acted as though I was doing *him* a favor for coming to visit.

I began our interview by explaining that "one of the things I loved about your story is that you're young, and you're figuring this out early on. A lot of the people I've interviewed started over in their later years and it took them a lifetime, almost, to realize that they could shift gears, completely change tracks, and be happier. What I found especially compelling about your story was that you're just a few years out of college and you've found it! Could you tell the story of when and how you started becoming interested in the global environment? And, first," for I simply couldn't hold it back, "how did you get the name Rhett Butler?"

Rhett smiled; the question about his name comes up almost every day. Rhett's grandfather had been the sole survivor of a military plane crash and had briefly roomed with Clark Gable (who played the original Rhett in the 1939 movie *Gone with the Wind*) as he helped Gable for his role in the movie *Test Pilot*. With that answered and out of the way, we moved on to my other questions.

Rhett's mother was a travel agent, so he had been privileged to travel the world as a child and teen. He told me that he had always loved the outdoors. As he put it, "I spent a lot of time alone as a child. I would go in the backyard and watch the ants or the birds or the bees and want to know more about them. My parents let me explore and ask questions." Traveling had, he thought, increased his natural interest in the environment. In traveling around the world, he was struck by environmental situations and inspired to know more. He realized that beautiful places were disappearing and wildlife along with them. "After seeing special places around the world, I'd think that it was too bad that other people wouldn't be able to see them because they won't be there anymore."

In high school, he began a project researching freshwater fish. Since he found no resource books that met his needs, he decided to create one. For two years, he met with people knowledgeable in the field, researched on his own, and developed a reference book. In the preface, he wrote a statement about the environment, and how people should think about where the fish came from. As he put it, "People don't realize that some of the fish that are pretty popular in aquariums are extinct in the wild now. Others are threatened . . . because people go out and collect them." A week after Rhett sold his book to a large aquarium publisher, the publisher was acquired by another company. If the new publisher hadn't printed the book by the end of seven years, rights returned to Rhett. Seven years and one day later, Rhett posted his book on the Internet for everyone to read for free.

Before Rhett started college, he took a trip to Malaysia and spent time in a beautiful rain forest observing orangutans and the richness of abundant tropical life. This trip and events that occurred soon thereafter were the inspiration for his next project, "A Place Out of Time: Tropical Rainforests and the Perils They Face." As he explained to me, "Eight weeks after leaving the tract of Malaysian rainforest that had filled me with happiness, I learned the forest was gone, logged for wood chips to supply a paper-pulp plant. This place of wonder and beauty was lost forever. . . . The loss of that small section of forest in Borneo created the urgency to act upon a thought that had been nagging me. While environmental losses and degradation of the rainforests have yet to reach the point of collapse, the continuing disappearance of wildlands and the loss of their species are disheartening. I feel sorrow for those who have not yet had the privilege of experiencing the magnificence of these places, and I try to picture how—should biodiversity losses continue to mount—I will explain to my grandchildren why these places that I enjoyed in my youth no longer exist."

Rhett's website provides an overview of the rainforest, its animals, and how the ecology works. It explains the deforestation that is happening and its consequences such as erosion, species lost, and climate-change related issues. Rhett also proposes solutions for the issues. It seemed to me that Rhett had already accomplished quite a lot in just a few years. Was he completely driven and focused throughout his life? I learned that was not the case, at least not in ways one might expect. As Rhett explained, in college, he had just done the average amount of work needed to pass. His passion was in his projects. He finished school a year early with a degree in management science. His strengths were in economics and math; his passions lay in biology and the outdoors. It wasn't very long before the consulting and investment banking world came courting Rhett for fast-track career possibilities. Why didn't he sign right up for these big salaries and prestigious offers?

Rhett told me that he had known what he *didn't* want to do: he didn't want to move to New York and he didn't want to become an investment banker and work eighty hours a week for something he didn't believe in. Since he had graduated a year early, he felt that he had been given a gift of time, an extra year in which to "figure things out." He decided to work on the rainforest project, postponing taking what he called a "real job." On some level, Rhett realized that he was also taking time to go within, time for reflection, time to discover more about himself. He spoke as though he had begun his year "off" with great enthusiasm and confidence in the process.

A year "off" is a luxury few can afford, so I wondered (and asked) how he had made money. Or had his parents supported him? He thought back for a moment before he responded. "Let's see," he said, "1998. I started trading commodity derivatives, such as cocoa, pork bellies, and corn. Then I developed a kind of standard deviation algorithm for trading. That did really well and I made a ridiculous amount of money. Then, I lost a ridiculous amount of money: $400,000." When trading proved too risky, he looked for other options using his analytical skills. As he said, "For some reason, I can look at a business plan and point out problems with it, so I earned some income doing that as well. This was during the heyday of the Internet and I earned a good salary staying in San Diego looking at those business plans for ten to twenty hours a week. I had the rainforest project on the side. The book about rainforests was going to help people learn about all of the issues. I wasn't hand-to-mouth financially, but it was all hard work."

He was expecting the Internet to crash and the economy to start collapsing. After careful thought, Rhett got a "real job" and began working with a small technology company run by people he knew. As he put it, "The company had a lot of potential and the guys developing it were producing an amazing technology. I was impressed with what they were doing. I also liked the guys who were running the company." Rhett worked hard and long days. And at the end of the day, he would go home to his rainforest project. Fairly late in the process, while the manuscript was in peer review, the potential publisher informed him they were not planning to include photographs, since that would make the book too costly. To Rhett, that undermined the point of the book. Then the thought came to him: "Why don't I just put it on the Internet? It's not that hard converting it from Word into a website. I am not technical at all, but I figured it out and did it." Rhett posted his book, giving something valuable to the world, with no expectation of a return for himself other than his passion for sustaining the global environment and the world's rainforests.

After 9/11, when there was such a scare about bioterrorism, he wrote an article about smallpox and posted it on the Internet. It was the first time he experienced significant Web traffic and the first time the search engines began crawls on his site. When he added fish content—including photos of fish in their natural environment—the site immediately became wildly popular with fish enthusiasts (who knew of him because of his website). It made for a lot of traffic on his site—but only about five dollars a month through Amazon referrals. Thanks to what he had learned at his day job at the technology company, he decided to put ads on his site, ads that were based on the page contents. Beginning in 2003, those ads began to generate significant income. By December 2003, Rhett's website had climbed rapidly in popularity and was generating more than his fairly hefty salary at the Internet company.

Rhett gave his day job six months' notice. He wasn't yet quite ready to jump off his cliff to do only the work he loved, but he was contemplating a whole different commitment. He was ready to believe that his passion and his life's purpose were connected. He was going to trust that the website would continue to support him at the level of his economic needs. I remembered my discussion with Terry Pearce about how when one is following the right voice, resources start to come; it seemed Rhett had found that place. On June 1, 2004, Rhett left the Internet company to devote himself full time to his website. He had jumped off the cliff. As he put it, "I quit my job and never looked back." Now, as he gave himself permission to commit fully to the work he deeply cared about, he became inspired and filled with energy and enthusiasm. He had always been driven to excellence in what he did, but this was more. Rhett's voice exuded passion as he said, "I just love what I do. Every day is my day off!"

I smiled and responded, "Every day is your day off because you are in your right work, and you can't believe you are getting paid to do something that feels so right?"

"Yes, basically that's right!" Rhett laughed and said, "It sounds like a good scam!"

"I know," I said, "that is what everyone who is in right work says. People feel they will be found out and then they will have to go and find a real job."

His face sobering just a bit, Rhett emphasized, "It's important though to know that it doesn't happen overnight; it takes practice and time. People think they can just put up a website about 'My dog' and then retire at thirty. It takes time and hard work."

Clearly Rhett knew about hard work. I asked, "Thinking back on your decision to quit your day job and give your notice, what gave you the courage to do that?"

"I saw that it was potentially viable," he said, "that I could earn the revenue." About a month after he quit the Internet company, another friend's company made an offer to Rhett, what he called "a ridiculous offer that was seven times my website income. It was a lot of money, but I would have been selling and sitting in a cube talking to tech people. That was my idea of hell." Even so, Rhett put the offer on hold, telling them he'd talk to them in six months. By the end of those six months, his website revenue had tripled. As he put it, "My income wasn't in league with their offer, but I knew that to take that job would have been selling my soul; I told them a final no." Since then, his site has just kept on growing. Rhett continued, saying, "It's been great. I meet all sorts of interesting people. Every day is different. I get to talk to people who are also following their passions, like scientists studying beetles somewhere, scientists doing exactly what they love to do."

Such enthusiasm! In my decades of recruiting, I'd met few people of *any* age—clients and candidates, alike—who exhibited such happiness, focus, and productivity. I could see that Rhett had stood in the lines for being conscious, sensitive, innovative, passionate, self-reliant, creative, tenacious, and courageous. I knew that, building on his passions and his upbringing, he had given himself permission at an early age to deepen his knowledge and experience about nature. He identified and used his strengths and acknowledged his weaknesses. As early as high school, he had thrown himself into researching the natural world, and continued to proactively teach himself what he needed to learn. In doing so, he deepened his knowledge and understanding of the world's rainforests and they became his life passion. Innately gifted with self-reliance and tenacity, Rhett strengthened both through solid economic dual tracking and years of research. He identified two of his goals to be helping change the way people think about the environment and helping to preserve some habitat and some species. From a young age, Rhett accessed and acted on his inner wisdom: he intuitively knew what he did *not* want to do for work and he respected his inner voice enough to listen to it instead of the voices of doubt and indifference from the outside world. I felt I knew a lot about Rhett—and I wanted to know more.

When I asked what was the one thing he would change if he had a magic wand, Rhett's answer was worlds apart from others I interviewed. He said that he would change the mindset that humans are separate and apart from nature. He feels that this paradigm is what allows us to ignore the enormity of our impact on the environment. His answer amazed me—and perhaps it shouldn't have. I could see that Rhett fully understood his gifts and his purpose in life and had found his right work, long since. He was living proof of the saying that each generation seems to get smarter earlier. My German grandfather, who said, "Ve get too soon alt and too late schmart," would have been pleased to meet Rhett Butler. As was I.

I asked Rhett, "If you had the opportunity to give counsel or advise people who had not a clue about what their right work was, but knew for sure what was their wrong work, what tips you would tell them are critical for success in finding their own right work?

Rhett thought for a moment, and said this:

- Be aware of what is going on around you, wherever you are. Be proactive. A lot of people are not happy with what they do, but they don't really look around at other options. Instead, it seems they like to complain more than look and act.

- Traveling and reading both give you a more open mind. If you can't afford to travel, you can always read about other places, cultures, different societies.
- Respect other people's opinions. Even if you think the person may not be right, know that it's just a different view.
- If someone tells you that you can't do something, that doesn't mean it can't be done. People get discouraged too easily. For almost any problem, there is usually a potential solution or a work around. I'm not going to say that nothing is impossible, but things that may seem impossible are still possible.
- Remember, experiencing a terrible product or service can be an opportunity for you to develop a better project or service.

He then added, "In high school, I probably thought I would be a scientist. I didn't know what the Internet was then and never thought I'd be doing what I'm doing now. I didn't set out to do this project. It happened. You can't plan out every step along the way; instead, you have to pursue what drives you and embrace the serendipity of life." As he paused for a moment, I thought about the points Rhett had made and how clearly they reflected a commitment to lifelong learning, self-reliance, respect for others, and acknowledgment of inner wisdom. He continued, saying, "I don't have a dialogue in my head—I just know."

Those last three words—"I just know"—resonated. On a certain level, Rhett could not have known early on what his work would look like. Why? Like so many other work and job opportunities today, it hadn't even existed fifteen years ago. In those years, the newly emerged "tail" of the Internet has grown in its breadth, reach, and potential for economic success. Yet in keeping with the universal law of attraction, the farther along Rhett marched on the path to his right work, the deeper his commitment and involvement, and the more success appeared. Clearly Rhett's outlook, training, and drive were serving him well.

One reason I had wanted to talk with Rhett is because what he's teaching is so critically important relative to the future. Rhett (who doesn't yet have children) had mentioned that his future grandchildren might not be able to even see a rainforest. As a grandmother myself, that statement touched my heart. My grandchildren are precious to me and I want a world for them that is as rich and whole as the one in which I've lived. And when Rhett made clear that he wants to contribute first and make money second, his voice echoed many of the most successful and fulfilled people I have met. I was reminded in particular of Robert Mondavi and how his eyes sparkled as he told me that his passion was in wanting to teach America about fine wines by making the best wines in the world. Robert too, cared first about the contribution he was making to others. For him, the money followed. There was no doubt in my mind that Rhett would have all the income he needed in his lifetime.

In many cases, environmentalists have seemed a bit on the fringe and very much to the left of business. But not Rhett. In his focus and with his rational and analytical thinking, Rhett is a practical visionary, perhaps a modern day, global John Muir. In the time since I first interviewed him, the reach and influence of his work has grown exponentially, reflected in the ever-increasing number of hits on his site: to ten million in 2010 and an average of 2.5 million visitors per month in 2011. As of this writing, his expanded sites are available in eight languages; the Mongabay websites for children, developed to interest and involve the next generation, are currently available in thirty-nine languages. Plus, his new children's book will be released in five languages. Day by day, hit by hit, Rhett's passion, combined with his skills and gifts are helping to raise awareness and support sustainability in the environment. Just as "Snorkel Bob cares," it is clear that Rhett Butler cares and is actively contributing his gifts to the world. What a blessing for endangered species, for the rainforest, and for all of us, that he came to this knowledge and calling so early in his life. He also serves as a role model for youth, showing just how much impact one person can have when they care about something passionately.

Rhett's attention to detail and his attention to the big picture, to the planet itself, brought me back to one of the many lessons from my long-standing conversations with Terry Pearce. Without a doubt, Terry exemplified the courage to jump off many cliffs, to move from his old work, his old life, his old beliefs, toward a new path, with an inner direction. I asked him what advice he'd offer to people who are looking for what it is they are to contribute in their lives at the level of their own gifts, a piece of advice he might give people as they begin the journey to knowing what they want to do.

"Above and beyond the Delphi oracle's advice of 'Know Thyself,' I assume." Terry said, smiling. "Just think what a magnificent incantation that was, and how difficult. So, once people know that it's important to know themselves, what would I say? There are many ways of knowing ourselves, ways that often don't have anything to do with our logical mind. Availing ourselves of those possibilities, whether it is through our dreams, our imagination, or through careful attention to the multiple messages that we get everyday from what I consider to be a gracious and loving universe. Training yourself to receive and to act on those messages is probably the most difficult and the most rewarding part of finding out who you are and what you're supposed to do. It's very hard, really difficult, perhaps particularly so for a Westerner."

"In my experience," I said to Terry, "I've seen that because of their fears—fear of not being able to pay the mortgage, fear of losing everything—many people don't step out from the tried-and-true path. What would you say of that?"

Terry took a moment and a breath before saying, "I have lost everything. So I understand that as a real fear. The important question we need to answer ourselves is what have we really lost, if we do? Are you more concerned about losing things or about losing your life and the meaning of it? Are you willing to live in a mediocre way in order to have an extra bicycle or an extra television set? Are you willing to come to the end of your life knowing that you made that choice? I would say the answer to that is probably not. So risking the things you have is not nearly as great as risking the loss of who you are. That's a philosophical issue. It's a decision that people have to make; it's part of what stepping out means. Have faith that the universe is going to provide. I know that sounds like an airy-fairy thing, but whether I have been in need or not in need, as long as I was on the right course, I have been provided for. The only time I felt like I risked losing everything is when I got off my path; that's when the resources disappear."

"Well," I said, "that brings up a very important point: there is a price for everything in life. And I believe that when you go on a journey like finding right work, it is truly the journey of finding a right life in terms of its expression. You have to be prepared to make certain sacrifices. For me, maybe it's around the discipline and financial sacrifices necessary to write this book. Or maybe it's around personal relationships. Or maybe it's about the willingness to be open to new ways of living that are not the traditional paradigms that other people understand. And all of that takes courage and a certain amount of thought. And I think that it's important to understand that this is not a cookie-cutter, one-size-fits-all process. This is a unique journey that we each make on our own. And it's going to have a price."

Terry nodded, saying, "The point about being alone and being an individual is really important—in a Western tradition. And this doesn't mean that we operate in a vacuum by ourselves and we're all Lone Rangers. Instead, in finding our unique shape, we're actually learning how to be with the whole. We're learning our place in the interdependence of it all, finding how we perfectly fit in. It's like discovering yourself as piece of the jigsaw puzzle: once you actually define the little courage and shapes of your own life then you fit into the total picture beautifully. So at the same time you're learning how to be alone, you're learning, as Brother David Steindl-Rast would say, that alone also says "all-one;" it also translates into all-one. So you're learning how to fit perfectly into the interrelated universe that we have. The more you develop and understand what your contribution is, the better you fit; the better you realize how interdependent we all are, the more you play your own individual role."

And then Terry returned to the price we pay, reminding me that "the price of the life you want is the life that you have." He added, "as you dream your life into being, as you dream and imagine the life that you could lead, there will be a time when you have to act and that means you have to leave the life that you have. There's no parachute, there is no ability to fly, there is no earth rising up to meet you until you jump. At that point, it's not the right thing, it's the only thing. That's exactly how I've felt."

Terry continued, "There is an old biblical story, one that probably has passed down from minister to minister, with a long history. The image it uses is that of the 'Hound of Heaven,' a powerful, unending force, following you and, much as Luke Skywalker's Force, moving you toward your salvation, moving you toward grace. It's the reason you do this thing. It's not like you have a choice between A and B, it's the Hound of Heaven moving you ahead in the direction you need to move."

We had talked about the changes Terry had made over the years. He had said that when he left IBM, it was a going away from; when he worked on the Initiative, when he established Leadership Communication, when he went to Schwab, when he went to graduate school, it was a going toward. Was that his Hound of Heaven chasing him away from some ventures and toward others?

He leaned in toward me, adding, "A dear friend of mine expresses it this way, 'There is a constant cycle, the contraction-expansion and contraction-expansion, the beating of the heart.'" It was a rhythm we both understood. I asked what further advice he might offer to people searching for their right work, searching for how to best use their gifts.

"I'd say we need to listen, to heed, to pay attention. Pay attention to everything. Pay attention to your aches and pains; pay attention to your dreams; pay attention to other ways of knowing. They're all around us, all the time; they're always available to us. Certainly the brain is important, and you can make that list of pros and cons of doing something, but the brain is not everything—and it's not a very good guide for fulfilling life by itself. Pay attention to everything."

"Oh yes," I added. "You know Zen story of a student who asked his master to write something of great wisdom. The Zen master picked up his brush and wrote the symbol for one word: 'Attention.'" Terry nodded in agreement as I continued: "And the student said, 'Is that all?' The master wrote, 'Attention. Attention.'"

Terry leaned back in his chair and said, "And there you have it. Attention. We are all given reminders to pay attention, and keep needing reminders, it seems. After his dystopian novel, *Brave New World*, Aldous Huxley wrote a final novel describing an entirely different, even utopian, society. For me, the message of that novel, *Island*, is captured in just those words, by the mynah birds who appear throughout the story, constantly calling out from the trees, singing: "Attention. Attention." That's what we're saying. And you know, in case we weren't paying enough attention, Huxley wrote of gratitude in that novel too, making reference to William Blake's statement that "Gratitude is heaven itself; there could be no heaven without it." Attention and gratitude. . . .

Coming from one whose inner voice is so strong, the advice to pay attention and to practice gratitude rings loud and clear. Terry has learned how to find right work multiple times over and exudes an ageless enthusiasm for life and work. He has built his life from courage, faith, discipline, and hard work. His contributions to his family, to his extensive and ever-growing network of friends, to his community, and to the world at large have yet to be measured. Terry knows that his work and life are a critical and valuable piece of an interconnected puzzle of cosmic design. He knows that his deepest purpose lives in the work he does that contributes to the higher good of others and to the highest good of the planet itself. All the more reason to listen and pay attention to that inner wisdom within.

Epilogue

We should know that all the Power in the Universe conspires to help us.

ERNEST HOLMES, AMERICAN THEOLOGIAN

In the beginning of the previous chapter, I alluded to the fact that the five steps to right work are interdependent and that inner wisdom illuminates them all. Finding, listening to, and nurturing your inner wisdom is, like each of the earlier steps, a continuing process and one that gets easier. With time. With practice. With increasing confidence in the true wisdom of your inner voice.

Inner wisdom. It's always there. Not just for those who have been on retreats or spent years practicing some special form of meditation. You don't have to practice a religion to hear inner wisdom or climb a mountain to hear words of wisdom from a guru who has spent a lifetime in retreat. You do have to pay attention. You do have to be open to new possibilities. You do have to be committed to becoming attuned to yourself separate from the world outside of you in order to learn to trust, fully hear, be guided by, and be able to fully incorporate your inner wisdom into your life and work.

Inner wisdom. The constant beat of the heart. With each interview, with each discussion I had in the course of gathering material and working on this book, I felt more committed to helping a broad range of people discover and live their right work. Every step along

119

the way became yet another reminder to pay attention—to pay careful attention—to both my inner and outer world.

It was not by coincidence that as I was working up the Action Items, the practical to-do lists in the next section, I saw that they logically fell into three groups. Some items require that you seek help from others (taking formal assessments, bolstering your skills, seeking others' opinions, interviewing people in areas that interest you): the outer work. There are some items that you have to work on by yourself (with encouragement and guidance from what I've written in the previous chapters and with continuing support online): the inner work. And some require that you've begun the outer and inner Action Items before you can properly work on them (clarifying your values and priorities, making full and appropriate use of your expanding network): outer and inner together.

As I pulled together stories and worked on developing concrete stepwise Action Items, I often drew lessons from the people I was actively helping to find right work and from the experiences of those I had placed in past years. I also drew lessons from my own life and from the very process of getting the journey of right work into words. I had many years of experience on which to draw. And I had been physically gathering notes for years, ever since an event I witnessed on a vacation.

I was visiting a small island off the eastern coast of Thailand, Koh Samui, where at that time no buildings were taller than a coconut tree. As part of my explorations, I attended a graduation ceremony of the most enthusiastic student body I have ever seen. It was my experience of this graduation that first inspired me to write this book.

The graduates had completed their training and put on an exhibition to showcase their acquired skills. Everything about their natural abilities and skills appeared to fit them like a glove. Their energy levels perfectly matched the demands of the job. Their seemingly natural talents made their accomplishments appear utterly effortless. Their abilities were well utilized, not stymied or thwarted. Most significantly, there was innate joy clearly present in their execution of the work itself. It was suddenly clear to me that 100 percent of the graduates were in their right work. Their enthusiasm was contagious. Their joy was palpable. These graduates had confidence in their abilities and I had no doubt that a positive, productive future for each graduate was assured.

There was no "Pomp and Circumstance," there were no caps and gowns, there were not even any diplomas. And yet, I was fully inspired by this Koh Samui graduation and the readiness of the graduating class. Never mind that these were monkeys who had been taught to pick brown coconuts, rather than those that were still green.

There, on vacation, I thought of the people I had met over my career as a search consultant, mentally scanning for those who exhibited anything close to this level of enthusiasm and happiness for their work. Happily, I found quite a few in my memory bank, in a wide range of work situations. While their work was much more complicated and demanding than picking coconuts, it had suited them perfectly. It seemed work they had been born to do, and their enthusiasm and energy for it was boundless. But of all the people I had met and worked with, this fit was nowhere near 100 percent of any graduating class, no matter what the school or the training level. I began to imagine what the world would be like if even a majority of human beings were working at such a high level of connection to their unique body of skills and talents. Just think what the world might be like if everyone could give their gifts to the world, if everyone could embody their unique talents in their work and in their lives.

So that's what inspired the start of this book, long ago. After my vacation, I went back to work, my right work, and whenever I thought of that ceremony on Koh Samui, I smiled to myself. Granted, people aren't monkeys and the scope of our right work is—to my mind— limitless. Limitless and ever changing. But there I was in my business, helping people, one person, one search at a time. I was enjoying it, making a good living doing it, and yet I knew I could help only some of those people who made it to my door. For some I'd have the right match in a job; for others, some tips that might help them uncover their right work; others needed more guidance and time than I could provide, particularly while running my business.

But that inner voice kept nagging me: I could do more, I could reach more people. My television production "Home Sweet Office" had helped me better recognize and share the steps that people took to find their right work; it was a start. And, in a way, the universe kept nagging me. Friends and clients often asked me to put my ideas about right work to paper or online, as a blog, so that they could have a portable coach and guidebook on this journey. I honed a larger number of steps down to the handful that I consistently saw in the people who were most successful in matching their talents to their tasks, in creating work that aligned with their priorities. I ran a few seminars, reaching more people. But my business (and my busy life) seemed to always take precedence over the wider outreach that a book and expanded website could provide.

In time, I began to wonder why it was taking me so long to truly commit to writing the book whose premise I was so passionate about. Why did I allow my search practice to take over and consume all of my energy? Why did I go so long without acknowledging and protecting enough space for the book on my calendar? What was preventing me from moving in the direction of this dream? Despite all the cliffs I had jumped off in my life and in my career, why was I procrastinating at the edge of this new cliff, year after year? Was it simply because of my own fear of failing and falling? And if so, why now?

Some lessons, it seems, I have to learn and relearn. Here, it seemed I was having to relearn lessons about fear, lessons that Jerry Jampolsky's book had helped me with so many years ago, and that Jerry himself had reinforced for me over the years. But this fear took a new form and required that I take that step again. And so it is with all the steps: the five steps to right work are not simply five discrete steps and you're done forever, set for life. These steps are part of a continuing journey: we cycle through steps again and again as we change, as circumstances change. The steps may look slightly different each time, sometimes even harder and steeper, but the self-awareness and wisdom available to take them grows over time. And the mental muscles, courage, and confidence needed are strengthened with each moment.

Over time, I found that with fear clearly visible in the picture, once I started questioning, more questions came pouring through that door. When had I been on or off the path? When had I had the courage to jump and where had I been stuck? I began to wonder if it was simply the nature of youth to jump more easily. That, I knew (because my inner voice told me) was an excuse. I knew many people who had jumped off of significantly bigger cliffs than committing to write a book all through their lives. You've read about some of them here and surely you know others.

My mind flashed on Terry Pearce and I realized that one reason I admired him so thoroughly was because he had been able to jump ever again as he followed his inner voice into deeper and deeper right work. He had spoken with me about his vision for himself and his business and how, at various points along the way he had stopped listening and nearly short-circuited his progress. It made me wonder: Had I stopped listening because of my fear?

Were all the roadblocks to writing this book a reflection of my own learning about the process of finding right work? Was there a metaphor for my own life hidden in there? Or maybe I was making it more complicated than it really was. Remember: the German part of my heritage and voices from my past (versus my true inner voice) tend to describe work as effortful. Those voices kept mumbling that if it's not a struggle, it's not valuable work. So some part of me had to make it hard?

But I knew that I had been in my right work for all these years and that much of my work—and often all of it—had seemed effortless and fun to me. I fully understood the refrain I hear from many people, the comment that Rhett Butler echoed: "I just love what I do. Every day is my day off!" And it's true: as you read in the stories in the earlier chapters, people in right work—no matter what their age—are inquisitive, lifelong learners; they have endlessly renewable energy levels; and, in living their passions, they accomplish extraordinary tasks, often more than they had imagined for themselves. Many of them have been in serial right work, work that evolved as their interests and skills changed and developed over the years. Right skills, right time, right work: it all comes together.

Like the monkeys in Koh Samui that first inspired me to write about right work, I have been in my right work and placing people in their right work for years. My business continues to draw on and is built upon my strongest talents and strengths. Each new search is a new challenge and I love the whole process. From interviewing new candidates to the long-standing relationships with many clients, it all challenges and renews me. But sitting all alone with the computer to write? Not so much.

Finally I realized it wasn't really the writing itself that scared me. Instead, I realized that what was keeping me from the book was a negative voice, one that I hadn't completely purged from myself. On some level, I thought, "All these other people can do fabulous things, things that ripple out far beyond their little spot on the planet. But me? Who's going to listen to what I have to say?" Never mind that plenty of people do, and have done so for years. That doubting voice doesn't hear reason. Instead, it whispered, "Out in the big, bad world of publishing, who will care about my purpose here and my book?" But I plugged on, trying to still that voice, as I wrote and then submitted a portion of the book and my proposal to a literary agent, one who had been recommended to me through a very successful author. Thrilled that the agent agreed to read it, I sent it off in a hurry.

Months later, I had a business trip to the East Coast and managed to add some time to my stay so I could meet the agent in person and talk with her about plans for my book. I was riding high, confident of good things. That negative, doubting voice of mine was well hushed. When I walked into her office and introduced myself at the front desk, the receptionist jumped up, shook my hand, and exclaimed, "Leni Miller? The Leni Miller? We love your book!" She then told me that the agent had just gotten back into the office and would be with me in a minute. When I was led into the office, the agent, who was sitting behind huge stacks of manuscripts, pushed a few of them aside to shake my hand as I introduced myself. That over, she turned back to her desk and mumbled "Lenny, Lenny, Lenny. Now where is your manuscript?" My name is pronounced like the quiet street: Lane-y, but it didn't seem like the time to correct her, so I kept mum. She found my packet, looked at it for a few seconds, refreshing her memory, looked up, and said, "Would you like me to tell you why your book would never sell?"

In disbelief I nodded mutely and she continued, in her clipped New York accent, saying, "OK! You're not famous. And you're not an expert in what you're writing about." Famous, I couldn't argue, but with nearly forty years of experience at the time in placing people in right work, I am an expert in the field and told her so. No, she countered, "You're an expert in identifying wrong work. But I like your writing and you California girls are so cheerful, here's what we should do." She then went on to delineate an entirely different book, one that did not draw on either my passion or my expertise. I can laugh at the absurdity of it now, but then, just those few words up-ended me. It was as if with one tiny push with the point of her stubby pencil, this woman had plopped me off my horse—and I didn't get back on again for years. Why? It's not that she was so right or so powerful as to block my book. It's that her dismissal echoed that negative voice I'd thought I had banished from my head and—in that moment—she validated all those negative thoughts. Her words and my unspoken fears—fears I'd denied or repressed—hurled me off the horse and off the track.

I should have known better. Deep down, I did know better. Certainly there are plenty of examples in the publishing world of famous authors who had doors slammed on them. Remember J. K. Rowling's address to the Harvard graduating class mentioned in chapter1? Without her faith and determination, Harry Potter would never have become a worldwide sensation. Long before that came Theodor Seuss Geisel (better known as Dr. Seuss) whose first book manuscript was rejected twenty-seven times, before someone at Vanguard Press saw fit to publish *And to Think That I Saw It on Mulberry Street*. Coincidentally (or not), I happened upon an article in *More* magazine by Kathryn Stockett, author of the bestseller *The Help*. In the article (published in May 2011), Stockett describes her persistence in submitting her manuscript to one agent and then another, and having each one reject it. Then, after three and a half years of rejections, the sixty-first agent snagged the book and sold it three weeks later to Amy Einhorn Books, a division of Putnam. Good luck, timing, a direct consequence of all Stockett's revisions over the years, or a combination? We'll never know. But it is clear that without Stockett's persistence and faith in her direction, *The Help* wouldn't have made it to the bookshelves—and then the movie theatres. (The article itself is from *The Best Advice I Ever Got: Lessons from Extraordinary Lives*, a Random House anthology edited by Katie Couric.) The fact that I happened upon Stockett's story just as I was writing this closing piece to my book felt like a bit of serendipity to me. I only wish I'd read something like it right after that crushing first visit with an agent.

But why have I spent so many paragraphs describing my publishing pitfall? This isn't a book about publishing; it's a book about discovering your right work, about finding the best way for you to share your gifts with the world. I've learned (and it's been a bit of a circuitous route) that once you still those negative voices, once you appreciate the value of your own gifts, once you feel inside that what you have to offer is truly worthy, that you can shine your light into the world.

Did a little voice in your head just whisper, "But I'm not like all those people she's written of; I don't have something big to give to the world. And even if I do, even if it's hiding in there, how am I going to support myself while I find it, nurture it, and get it ready for the big time?"

Does it help to know that we all grapple with those voices, that even the most successful people have doubts? If your doubts sound anything like, "This comes so easily to me, how can it be real? How can this work have such value if it's so easy for me? Shouldn't this be hard? What if what I have to offer is not really valuable after all? My talents seem so paltry compared to (fill in your own blank); can it be worthwhile? Does the world really need what I want to give? What if mine is the wrong talent at the wrong time? Will I have enough (money, energy, support)?" you are not alone. I've heard these doubts and many like them from people just starting out, from people in midlife trying to discover their right work and their purpose in life, from people starting over; I've heard them across the desk and across the Internet.

Shush that voice and listen to my voice for a second. Or listen to my grandmother who, in reminding me of those lines in heaven, was linking me to wisdom that has been passed on through the ages.

Quieting those negative voices in your head so you can hear—and trust—the inner wisdom of your heart and from the universe takes faith and practice. And that's much of the purpose of the Action Items that follow. They will help you make progress on discovering your true talents and priorities and linking your life's work to them. Bit by bit, as you work your way though the Action Items, you will find that your inner wisdom comes through more often and more strongly; it is as though the connection to your inner power gets more finely tuned. And, just like a Wi-Fi connection, it can drift in and out a bit. Sometimes there's interference from others, from the media, from the general crush of life. There's no doubt that to hear and heed your inner wisdom you need to practice. That's where the quiet time and the mental fitness practice described in the Action Items come in. Think of the Action Items as your password for access to inner wisdom and your mental fitness practice as your way of connecting to the source.

My hope is that this book will help you recognize and be inspired to access your own strength—and the greater guidance you will receive. I know that it works. Not only have I helped people leap off cliffs into new directions that were the right fit for them and at the right time, I have jumped myself, multiple times. The nursing student who walked the leg to the morgue and herself right out of nursing school? That was me, long ago. Yes, I'd have done that differently with the knowledge I gained over the years. But there is no doubt that leaving nursing was the right choice for me. As was my decision (made slightly less hastily) to move back to San Francisco. Over time and with practice, I learned how to listen better and prepare better. I know, through my personal and professional experiences, that by stilling your mind through self reflection, you will become more self aware and you will begin to know how to access your greatest talents. Through self reflection, you will connect with the guidance that will lead you to more resources. And— as many people will attest but rarely print—through self reflection and awareness you can then recognize and receive still greater gifts.

Were I to write up all, or even a fraction of, the times that I have listened to my inner wisdom, asked for guidance from the universe, and had what I needed or wanted appear, you might dismiss me, saying, "Oh, sure. But she's in California; we don't believe that in (your state or country here)." But where you live now or where you were raised doesn't matter; what does matter is that guidance is there for all of us.

For me, the results have been amazing, some so much so that for years I hesitated to tell people. But you've read this far and already read some of them. Remember the apartment that was miraculously offered to me in San Francisco after I moved west with my two-year-old daughter? That apartment was remarkable on many levels, not the least of which is I was able to pay my landlord in conjunction with my commission checks. As it worked out, there were some months when I had no commission income, others when I had a healthy windfall. Not only had Paul Sing offered me just the apartment I needed at the time (and offered it when I had no job at all), he was fine with taking no rent some months, trusting (and knowing) that I would pay him as soon as the commissions came in.

Years later, when my daughter was getting ready to start school, I had assumed she'd be able to attend the wonderful public school practically across the street. But no, that was when children were being bussed great distances to help achieve racial balance across the school system. No matter what the school, I didn't want my five-year-old spending hours on a school bus. But I certainly could not afford a private school; I couldn't even afford a car. I asked for guidance. And then I received a healthy tax refund and used it to buy a car. Before I took my very first drive across the Golden Gate Bridge, I asked for guidance about what I should do, what would be best for my daughter and for me. I'd had enough experience to know to listen, but I surely didn't expect guidance to come right away. What happened? Once I was over the bridge, I suddenly knew I had to get off at the Tiburon exit; I listened to the voice. When I came to Cecilia Way, I knew I had to turn left and head up the hill. There, at the top, on Andrew Drive, I heard the sound of children playing in the swimming pool of an apartment complex. That surely was a good sign, since I had already discovered that many apartment complexes back then did not allow children. I parked and went into the office to ask about apartments. The woman behind the desk seemed a bit surprised by my request, said that there were rarely any vacancies at all but that just an hour before I walked in, a tenant had given thirty days' notice. Would a two-bedroom apartment suit me? Would it? I couldn't have asked for more: a separate bedroom for my five-year-old daughter, a pool out back with plenty of happy children, and a great school nearby. I could give my landlord the notice he needed and be settled well before school started. The biggest bonus, one that I didn't discover or fully appreciate until we had moved in, was that there were other single mothers in the complex and we became a solid community, helping each other with our children and supporting each other emotionally.

Surely I'd never call myself a better, more organized, more savvy apartment shopper than anyone else. To the outside world it may look as though I accidentally found that apartment (and the one before). To my mind it was no accident. I wound up where I was because I had focused on what I needed and I listened for help. Years down the road I used the same process, along with some of the practical Action Items, to focus my attention and wishes, and wound up (as you'll read later) owning a fabulous home, where I now live and work, all with a view of San Francisco Bay and Mount Tamalpais.

And while people would be free to call my housing finds pure luck, when they see others do extraordinarily well in business or in their chosen line of work, instead of luck, they often ascribe it to some remarkable gift, a personal greatness their own negative voice says they simply don't have. If you think the people I've written about in *Finding Right Work* are special or better than you in some way (smarter, luckier, more connected, having that special something that only a few are blessed with) believe me: that special something exists for all of us. Once you know and access your gifts—abilities that, for most of us were neither reinforced nor taught—you'll experience it for yourself. You can create anything you want or need. I know this, and yet I've had moments and even years of forgetting (witness all the years I had this book on hold, shoved to the back of my desk and my mind—but never abandoned). I also know that the life we have tomorrow is a reflection of our thoughts and actions today. So set yourself reminders, know that your unique talents and strengths are there, and that the world needs and wants them. Like the people whose stories you have read here, as you commit to using your gifts, you will find you have increasing happiness and energy and therefore increased contributions in your work. There may be bumps along the way (you've read about those, too), but they're part of growth and change. It's knowing yourself and having faith that the right answers will come that makes all the difference. Trusting in that inner wisdom supports you in the leap. With patience and practice you'll be guided in the right direction and to your right work. You will find that the world then supports you with the income, the living situation, and the community you need. Embrace change and move forward confidently, into your right work. Pay attention and you will find your answers.

Just recently as I was flipping through a book on a friend's coffee table, a quote leapt out at me: "The universe is change; our life is what our thoughts make it." A few days later, a friend who lives on the other side of the country shared the same quote, knowing it would strike a chord with me. I took it that it was time for me to really pay attention to the quote—from Marcus Aurelius Antoninus (CE 121–180). Clearly embracing change and constructing our lives through our thoughts is not a New Age invention, but a lesson for every age.

Be like those you've read of who found their right work. Be like those who, once they identified their strengths, values, and priorities discover that their work takes off. Whether it's in the cause of art, fish, the rainforests, wine, investments, special needs children, communication, possibilities for peace, right work, or your own favorite cause, the world needs you. Take this as an invitation and obligation to contribute your talents to the world. Create time and focus, pay attention, go within. Still your inner voices of doubt and listen to your inner wisdom. Find ways to develop your gifts and share your talents. Your talents are uniquely yours; no one else has your exact configuration of talents. The world needs your contributions. Commit your treasures and talents to make the world a richer place. Start with the Action Items. Don't put them on hold or push these explorations to the back burner. Get started on discovering what is truly your right work at this time in your life! I guarantee that when you do find your right work, you will create a life you love. If I can do it, so can you.

Action Items

H ere you are, at the beginning of the Action Items. If you've finished the main chapters of *Finding Right Work*, you've already read about people who are living in their right work, people who are living lives they love. You've seen each of the five steps—Jump, Let Go, Assess Your Talents and Skills, Identify Your Priorities and Values, and Trust Your Inner Wisdom—in action in many different circumstances. You've seen the whole picture, read about the success people have had in creating right work, and are ready to take action of your own. Or maybe you've just begun reading the book, know that you learn best by doing, and have decided to get started on the Action Items as you read about and absorb the five steps to right work, one at a time.

Whichever way you've gotten here, by addressing these Action Items and completing them, you will be moving forward, moving toward work that is right for you and toward your own best way of creating the life you love—all the while increasing your own happiness. Congratulations for choosing to actively manage the project of identifying your top priorities and strongest values and talents on the journey to finding right work.

The Action Items are focused, small practices that you can master, day by day. They are designed to reprogram your way of thinking as they guide you through the process. There are three sets of Action Items, grouped by type of activity.

1. *Prepare to Be Prepared* focuses on information from the world outside of you. For brevity, these are what we call the outer Action Items.

2. *Take Time for Reflection* focuses on identifying and changing the internal workings of your mind: your beliefs, self-talk (what you might tell yourself as you're reading about other people's success or checking out the Action Items), and access to self awareness, along with habits of action and thought that you've acquired over the years. These are the inner Action Items.

3. *Identify and Find Your Right Work* is designed to bring it all together, to help you integrate the first two sets. This set helps you use both the outer and inner and aspects of what you've discovered to accelerate your discovery of right work. These are the outer-inner Action Items.

Exactly how you take the steps to right work and begin the practice of the Action Items will be unique to you. The amount of time and effort you need to devote to practice will directly relate to where you are on your journey. No matter what your stage, the order in which you read chapters and work through specific Action Items is your choice. Many of the outer and inner steps can be done in parallel, more or less simultaneously with each other. That's true, with one caveat: my experience has taught me that people make the smoothest progress, the most consistent progress with minimal frustration or backtracking if they cover at least a major portion of the first two sets of Action Items before taking on the third set. That last group of Action Items (outer-inner together) works at the most effective level if you have already addressed significant portions of the outer work and the inner work.

My recommendation? Make a commitment to mastering all of the Action Items. Dedicate as much time as is possible every day to the project and take one day at a time. Don't allow your mind to think about the big picture. Stay present to and focused on your daily practice, whatever size it is. By moving through these lists, in which the tasks ahead are broken into specific Action Items, you will move forward, day by day. The more you do, the more you'll be strengthening your awareness and insight, the sooner you'll know your priorities, values, innate talents and gifts—and the sooner you'll know how best to use them in the development and discovery of right work. Working on these Action Items will strengthen your connection to your inner guidance, deepen your confidence, and inspire insights. Each one you practice will support the one that follows.

Icons in the outside margins tie to the chapters. If, for instance, you're reading chapter 2 and wondering how you can help yourself let go of needing to know, you can find the icon for chapter 2 and start right in on some specific tasks that will help you with that step. Just remember the earlier caveat: hold off on the outer-inner Action Items until you've worked on the outer Action Items and the inner Action Items.

As I've coached people, I've seen that real life stories of change and growth often inspire people to reach higher than they might alone. For that reason, I've interlaced several boxes among the Action Items. These are of two kinds:

- Reminders of a person whose success with the action item under discussion was described in an earlier chapter.
- New stories to reinforce the effectiveness and impact of the action item indicated.

As you practice the Action Items in the following pages, you will see that each set includes a progression of short, manageable exercises. These practices will lead you to more and more awareness (and longer strides), so that one day you will find that you have increased clarity about what is important to you at this point in time and you will know when you are ready and willing to jump off whatever cliff is ahead. You will have more and more faith in your own inner guidance and will begin to see how your personal priorities, values, and strengths will be reflected in your own right work.

1

Prepare to Be Prepared
Outer Action Items

This first set of Action Items focuses on gleaning information from external resources in the world outside. The first thing you need to do is prepare for that world by practicing specific, small steps day by day. Change happens more easily in small increments, and your commitment to actively work on the smaller Action Items is a critical component for success in the bigger picture of the steps to finding your right work. Now it's time for action and change. Yours.

Think about how you want to go about learning and taking the bigger steps to discovering your right work. The personal routes to right work are unique and they all emerge from the same five steps. The precise order of the steps themselves is also personal, and you'll want to incorporate some of the steps throughout your life. For instance, checking in on your priorities relative to work is as important as your annual physical or keeping tabs on your credit.

I've gone through this process—steps and Action Items—multiple times myself and I've coached people through the process over the years. So trust me when I urge you to put these Action Items right at the top of your list, to do first.

TAKE THE SMALL PRACTICAL STEPS

To implement this project, you need to carefully create the time and organize a system that will support your process of discovering right work. In these outer Action Items, you will get started and begin to get a better sense of what's ahead. For now, you are taking the preparatory steps to create a map and project plan for your journey. Many people spend more time than this in planning a special vacation; think of this as planning for life experience that will be much more meaningful and enduring than even the best of vacations.

MAKE THE TIME

Commit a defined amount of time in your day dedicated exclusively to the project of finding right work. Every day. Through each of the steps and each of the Action Items—from the mechanics of keeping track of observations, insights, and information as well as delving into your inner work— each step and each action item requires time and attention.

- ➤ How much time you devote is up to you, your budget, and just how quickly you want to find your right work.
  - If you don't have work and need income while you determine your right work, it's best to find contract or temporary work while you are on the path to discovery. Don't let the urgency of financial pressure undermine the commitment to find right work.
  - If you are not working now and don't need additional income, consider this project as your full-time commitment to work. Give yourself a certain period of weeks or months during which time you will gain clarity as to what is your right work.
  - If you do have work and are staying with it until you discover what is next, think of this project as your second job. Carve out time every weekday and even more on the weekend.
- ➤ Commit to the time—one hour, two hours, three hours—you'll devote to this a day. (You can always revise it up or down.) I recommend a minimum of sixty minutes per day as an initial commitment to the project.
- ➤ Take a moment, right now, to get that time on your calendar.
  - Divide it into two, three, or even more chunks if that will make it easier to fit into your calendar—and make sure it is in times of the day when you're most productive and clear.
  - If your calendar is already full and you need to find more time, look at what's on your calendar and what else creeps into your day. How do you spend your time?
    - ◦ Begin to see your project of finding right work as a top priority.
    - ◦ Identify activities you can cut back on, delegate, or drop to make time for this most important project.

- Are there some activities you could move to less productive times of the day to give this project more of your energy?
- Liberate time by saying "No" to activities that don't support your project of finding right work. Until you say "No" to activities and people that don't support the project, the "Yes" for your future cannot show up.

➤ Congratulations. You've already established a proactive focus and created a strong intention to change your old habits of mind and subsequent inertia from running your mind and your life. You've committed time to devote to the five steps to right work and to create a life you love.

ESTABLISH A SYSTEM TO MANAGE THE PROJECT AND RECORD YOUR JOURNEY

You'll need a portable, accessible way to keep track of all that you're doing and learning as you work through the steps and the Action Items. There will be a workbook available through this book's website. Or you may find it effective to create your own personalized system that you're sure to use. You'll be adding to it and consulting it throughout the project, so make it something you will enjoy, that will be easy to maintain and access.

Finding Right Work includes a wealth of advice, supplemented on the website (www.findingrightwork.com). It can be a virtual partner for you on this journey as you become your own personal project manager, your very own mentor and guide. Your record keeping system is an active metaphor for your intention to find right work. Writing ideas and thoughts down creates a different impact on the mind than just thinking and observing. By committing your epiphanies and insights to paper (or computer files) you're able to observe, review, remember, and anchor your changing perceptions.

Successful career consultants, human resource managers, search and job placement professionals have to be organized, resilient, tenacious, and dedicated as they manage high volumes of information, people, and ideas; you need to be also. The more you dedicate your time, your resources, and your focus to your personal project of getting to know who you really are at this moment in time, the more clarity you will develop about the parameters of your right work. The more clarity you have, the more easily you can say no to wrong work and the faster your right work will arrive. The faster your right work appears to you, the less time you will waste on wrong work and the happier you will become. The happier you become, the more you will love the life you are living.

> Create an easy and comfortable system for documenting your thoughts, experience, names of people, and resources for yourself. Make sure that it is a system you'll be consistent in using. You'll need a way to write things down wherever and whenever you have a relevant thought and a way to organize information as you gather it.

- Whether it's a loose-leaf notebook, a laptop computer, a smart phone, or a mini notebook in your pocket and a file drawer at home doesn't matter; the fact that you use it and update it every day does.

- Be sure it's practical for you. Maybe you don't carry a briefcase. You can always take notes in something that fits in your pocket, whether it's a mini notebook or your cell phone.

- Whether you sync your phone and computer or you manually enter your notes into your file system, be sure to make this step part of your day. You want to be able to capture your thoughts, your ideas, your research, your contact information. Every day.

> What's the best system for you? Take the time now to select it and begin.

> What folders and dividers will you need to keep track of the information that will come to you? Start with sections for professional assessments; assessments from friends, family, and associates; your career autobiography; your mission statement; career brainstorming; your network, both known and developing. As you get closer to your right work, you'll create sections on that field as well.

> Set this up and keep it front and center in your workspace at home and in your mind. The constant reminder will reinforce your commitment.

> Be sure to label your file. Whatever you choose, whether it's "Creating a Life I Love" or as simple as "Finding My Right Work," putting your

intention into print and seeing it will be a constant reminder that reinforces your commitment.

EVALUATE YOUR CURRENT WORK

Take a careful look at your current work situation relative to your priorities, values, and strengths. What is right about it? What is wrong about it? Assess your financial needs and what is necessary to keep body and soul together as you undertake your search for right work. Have you recently finished school and begun looking for that first job? Are you working full time, part time, as a consultant, contractor, or permanent employee? Have you retired from the military or a long career? Or are you not currently working? Each has obvious relevance as to how you customize this process.

➤ Are you currently working?

• If you are now employed by clients or by a company, you'll need to plan to take time for finding your right work without shortchanging your current work commitments and without leaving clues that make your employer or clients wonder if you will continue to give them your full attention.

• It is possible that in proceeding through your complete evaluation (Outer, Inner, Outer and Inner together), you'll realize that your current work has the potential to evolve into your right work. As this awareness becomes clear, as your attitude shifts, you may find that you are in fact in right work. Even if that's not the case, if your current work funds your effort for discovering and finding your true right work, it is a kind of right work—for the moment.

• Create time dedicated to your project that doesn't detract from your paid work commitments. You'll be amazed at how much you can get done in small increments if you are committed to staying with the project. Remember your enthusiasm for planning a well-earned vacation and generate that level of energy for discovering what your right work is at this stage in your life.

• If you choose to tell people about your project, do so with brevity, clarity, and care. Be aware that there is a tendency for others to

141

sabotage projects like this with their own projection of impossibility thinking. As Elsa Joy Bailey has said on her blog, "Don't let other people's opinions burn holes in your dreams."

➢ Are you not currently working?

- Do you have a financial cushion that enables you to make discovering and finding your right work your full-time interim job?

- Stop looking for a new job or new work for at least thirty to sixty days. Looking for something when you don't know what it is you are looking for is a fast track to discouragement and confusion.

- Consider economic dual tracking if you know your financial cushion won't last long. For inspiration, think of Marnie Walker (chapter 3), who kept her day job until her new business could support her and her family, and Rhett Butler (chapter 5), who developed his website after work hours.

- No financial cushion? Or a very slim one? Now's the time to take on contract, temporary, or interim work so that you can support yourself while you pursue this process. Short of coming into a sudden financial windfall, your best bet is to find work that pays you the most for the least amount of effort. This allows energy left over for the project of finding right work.

CREATE INTENTION AND BEGIN TO SHARE IT

Going public with the fact that you are undertaking the task of discovering right work requires planning and skillful communication. Whether you're undertaking this quest full time or part time, how you present your project to your immediate world (friends, family, associates) matters, and will directly impact the kind of response and support or lack of support you elicit from them.

➢ Answer your own questions first. Be certain you can answer the following questions with conviction and brevity before you share your intention with friends and family.

- Are you firmly committed to discovering your current right work?

- Are you prepared to get to know yourself at a more authentic level than ever before?
- Have you given yourself full permission to create a life you love?

➤ Get ready for sabotage and questions. Well meaning friends and family can lure your mind quickly backwards into fear and doubt. Whether a friend sees you reading this book or a relative notices you're asking more questions about work and life, you will soon be fielding questions about what you're up to.

  - Come up with a plan for when and how you'll share the fact that you're starting the steps to discovering your own right work. Questions to consider before you begin discussing your process relate to your personality, current employment, and ways of communicating with your network (work associates, friends, family, acquaintances).
  - If you're a very private person, or if you're surrounded by naysayers (you know the type: people who would undermine your plans and fill you with doubt instead of encouragement), you'll probably want to undertake the beginning steps completely independently, including reading this book privately. You'll not share what you're doing until you've developed confidence in the process and see that you are making forward progress.
  - But unless you are on a solitary retreat, you will be asked. So be ready. Come up with a simple line about the project. You'll want a positive, brief statement of intention that feels right to you. This statement will evolve over time. A few examples of what people have used in this early stage follow:
    - ○ "I'm taking time to discover my next right work."
    - ○ "I've launched a project of finding my right work."
    - ○ "I'm researching what work I want to do next."
    - ○ "I'm taking a sabbatical so that I can identify my next right work."
    - ○ And for someone a little closer to knowing her field, "I'm exploring how I might best use my experience and talents to help preserve the environment."

> Practice saying your statement of intention to yourself. Saying it out loud creates a strong intention and will help guide you. And if it doesn't ring true, you'll hear that and can modify it until it's right.

- Practicing creates strength in conviction for your project and boosts your energy about it. Plus, practicing before you go public will help you speak with confidence when it's time.
- A few tips will help make you comfortable saying your intention and projecting it positively, without hesitation:
  - Practice, practice, practice.
  - Say it in front of the mirror.
  - Say it to a person very close to you who is a supportive ally.
  - Visual reminders offer critical help. Write your statement down and place it in spots you (and only you) see often: your refrigerator door, your bathroom mirror, as your screen saver, in your wallet, by your bed, on the seat of your car.
- Once you've practiced your statement and are confident with it, sure that it is clear, precise, and positive about your goals for this initial phase, it's time for the next step.

PREPARE ANSWERS AND PAY ATTENTION

Very soon, you'll be ready to express what you're doing with a wider circle of people. Your professional and personal networks will become invaluable resources for your journey. Now that you have a clear and authentic response ready when others in your life ask what it is you are "doing," you'll find that their questions may well bring you answers, contacts, and ideas to explore as you progress along the path towards your right work.

> When a trusted friend or family member asks what you're up to, you could start an ongoing conversation. Help comes along when we least expect it. Who knows? The person you are talking to may be longing for his own right work too. You could end up partnering with one another and offering mutual support and help.

> As you branch out from your inner circle of trusted friends and family, you'll adjust what you say and how much you reveal.

- If you are currently an employee, be circumspect in your sharing, and maybe even consciously keep these conversations out of the workplace. You need to be careful that news of your journey not get back to your employer or clients if that would endanger your relationship or job. Some employers, however, are extremely supportive of and helpful to employees exploring both external and internal options for career development and discovery of right work. Take a careful read on the culture of your workplace and you'll know if yours is one of them.

- When someone you've just met asks the all-too-common "What do you do?" question, you have the opportunity for a helpful conversation. In addition to saying what you're doing, in asking about what the other person is doing, you can learn about other fields, interests, and possibilities. You may be surprised at the respect people express when you tell them that you are on the path to discovering your right work. Statistically, more than 80 percent of working people are not happy in the job they are in; chances are you'll talk to one of them. Pay attention and you will learn a lot. You could even find an important piece to the puzzle you're solving.

- Once you're proactive with your project and you are letting more and more people know that you're on the path to your right work, you will begin to experience the magic of "being in the flow" and begin to find increased numbers of relevant people and information coming to you.

- In time you may want to talk with some associates (outside of work) but there's more to do first (here, in these Action Items and in the inner Action Items). Getting beyond the first, fairly generic statement of intention requires inner work. As you make progress, your short statement will more clearly reflect the parameters of your right work and become more and more clear and concise. Then others will better know how they might help you.

- Listen to feedback and pay attention. Above all, be prepared for varying reactions when you begin sharing the idea of discovering right work.
  - You may think you know who will be supportive and who will be skeptical—and you may well be surprised.

- Stay open to the reactions you'll get and learn from them. Don't let people's reactions derail you. Instead, pay attention to the words without reacting to them and not taking anything personally. Assume there is something to be learned and heard in every response, even those that appear negative.
- Learn to listen to comments and your internal reactions without judgment or defensiveness. Begin to observe your own mind and its habits that have been programmed by culture, family, or others.
- Every time you talk about your journey, you'll learn something about yourself and others. Every time you express your intention, you will strengthen your resolve.

➤ All of this information—what others say and how you process their statements—is useful. Be sure you're writing down thoughts and ideas and adding the new information to your notebook or computer system.

3 GATHER INFORMATION ABOUT YOURSELF

Beyond hearing feedback about your statement of intention, you'll want to research and glean information about your beliefs, priorities, strengths, and weaknesses. You'll start with what you know for certain about yourself. You'll add in information from family, friends, colleagues, even former employers. You'll get another perspective from professional assessments, whether in person, online, or through books. Your goal is fact finding: you want to gather information about yourself from more effective self reflection, from those who know you well, and from those who are professionals in helping people assess their strengths and weaknesses. If you find yourself reacting emotionally or physically to any of the questions, take note of that and write a quick note about your reactions as a reminder.

REFLECT

➤ Values, strengths, talents, and priorities. Take some time to sit down in a quiet place and begin to identify information about what you perceive to be your core life values, your strongest gifts, talents and skills, and your top five to ten priorities relative to work.

- Be thoughtful and honest with yourself as you do this. There's no one watching. There are no wrong or right answers. No one else will read it. Let yourself write without editing or critiquing as you go.
- Keep it free form. You will revisit this later and can organize and add to it then. If you're using a paper notebook, be sure to allow plenty of space so you'll have room to add more thoughts later on.

➤ Past and present work experience. List all the work you have done, either consulting or as an employee, full-time or part-time, in your field or outside of your field. For each experience, write down the following:

- Projects and activities you've enjoyed the most. Write whatever comes to mind. Stay open to it.
- An inventory of what you're proud of and your accomplishments. Remember the times when you were very happy in work and what about it makes you feel good when you remember it.

➤ If you are recently out of school and do not yet have much work experience, simply write up any project, internship, or other work experience you have. You have learned more than you might have thought, even from part-time work as a teenager. Some of those early jobs help us define what we don't want to do, in addition to giving clues as to what we're good at and will want to pursue. For each experience, write down the following:

- Projects and activities you've enjoyed the most. Write what comes to mind.
- Other projects that looked interesting to you, projects in which you'd liked to have participated.

➤ Education. Formal and informal, past, present, and future. When you've covered your work experience, think of your years of formal or informal education and areas of study. Remember the subjects you most loved and the classes you most enjoyed and in which you did well. Think ahead to any studies or training you're anticipating. If you aren't academically inclined, recall the nontraditional education and learning you've experienced. Take note of what was most interesting to you.

Revisit the same steps you've just covered, listing projects and activities you've enjoyed the most, during your informal or formal education, including any training classes or seminars.

➢ Volunteer experiences. Think of volunteer activities, of all kinds, in which you've been involved over the years. List them all and take note of what was meaningful to you and what was it you enjoyed about them. Be as specific as possible.

- Are there any volunteer activities that you always remember? What makes them memorable?
- Are there any volunteer activities that you've wanted to do, or hope to devote more time to at some point in your life?

➢ Hobbies. List your hobbies and interests. Include what you are active in today, in earlier years, and even hobbies you might like to begin. For each, think about (and write down) what draws you to them.

➢ Avocations, vocations, or professions. List all that you've been drawn to or ever considered. Go all the way back as far into your childhood as you can remember. Did you once want to be an actress or actor? Write it down. Anything that has interested you is worth adding to this list. Look back over what you've recorded and double check.

- Did you include your years in school?
- Did you include all of your work experience? Everything?
  - ○ Part-time teenage jobs?
  - ○ Part-time jobs in college?
  - ○ Temporary jobs?
  - ○ Contract jobs?
  - ○ Everything all the way up to your current work?
- Did you reflect on other relevant aspects of your life, from childhood to the present day?
- Were there any surprises?
  - ○ Were you surprised to find that childhood interests popped up in your mind as frequently as your recent undertakings?
  - ○ Did you feel you had to think hard for certain categories?
  - ○ Whatever surprises you encountered, take note.

Later, in the inner Action Items, you'll make use of these lists and expand on them still more. For now, just allow yourself to think back over your life to date and make note of those times you were absorbed completely in the activity or those things you have been dreaming about, picturing yourself doing. Whenever something bubbles up from memory, add it to the lists you've now started.

GATHER

In parallel (and without sharing what you've already learned about yourself), seek information from those who know you well. You'll be asking for information from a wide variety of people. Be sure to include people who know you the best. Come up with a list of at least ten people who know you well and who would respond to your request for feedback about your personal and professional strengths and assets, weaknesses, and even foibles.

> - Who should you include?
>   - Family: immediate, extended, parents, older and younger relatives.
>   - Friends: old friends and new friends. You don't need to ask everyone, but you should aim for a balance from different stages of your life and for different ages of responders. A coaching client of mine included a twelve-year-old neighbor in her list and received some very valuable insights.
>   - Associates, colleagues, and acquaintances: current and past work, people in your neighborhood, volunteer partners, members of your spiritual community, former employers, and fellow employees.
>   - Be sure you're not self-selecting to get only favorable responses. Knowledge of weaknesses, which are many times the flip side of strengths, is very valuable and can provide important insights for your next steps.
> - What to do? Assuming you are tackling this action item early in the process, your request should be open ended. Be sure to share that you want their honest input relative to your strengths, talents, and weaknesses. Explain that you are beginning the project of discovering your

current right work and that the feedback they offer will allow you to know yourself better. Ask them for their perception of

- your strongest talents, abilities, skills, strengths;
- your weaknesses and blind spots; and
- your most significant contribution to their lives.

➢ How you present your request and approach people is important so that people are comfortable with this step. Naturally, you'll want to personalize this request for each person you contact.

- Be sure that you are comfortable with asking people. You may want to ask only your closest family and friends first before you branch out to others.
- Be certain that people understand that you want honest and thorough input.
- When you start receiving input, remember you're receiving unique perceptions. Pay attention to themes that appear and reappear. Who you really are is a discovery you will make at several levels deeper than this feedback.

RESEARCH

A variety of tools are used in professional assessments, designed to expand your self knowledge and help determine the types of work in which you can make good use your natural talents and skills, the type of work for which you are naturally suited. Businesses also use some of these assessments to help put together teams whose members will work well together and complement each other's strengths.

➢ The Myers-Briggs Type Indicator (MBTI) assessment has been in use since its introduction in 1962. In my experience, it has been by far the most popular assessment in business for many years. It classifies cognitive functions, helping to illuminate how individuals absorb new information, make decisions, and interact. Executives tend to know their Myers-Briggs types as well as, if not better than, their body weight. For many people, learning their Myers-Briggs type has provided breakthroughs in understanding at both a personal and professional level.

Detailed explanations and short versions of the assessment itself are available online for free. There are also books about everything from team building with types to hiring for types.

➢ Cathy Caserza-Light, the founder of Assessment Leaders LLC, fully understands the benefits that assessment tools can provide, both for companies looking to hire and for individuals discovering their own right work. As she put it, "You have the talent to be exceptional in some role or task. The trick is for you to find that 'something' where you can shine. Your self-assessment can give you a head start." Since companies are increasingly using assessment tools, it makes sense to use some yourself, "to know as much about yourself as possible so that, ultimately, you're going after the right work or job that fits you." She recommends two tools in particular, tools that are also often used by companies in their pre-hire assessments.

  • ProfileXT is a fifty-minute "total person" assessment that measures job-related qualities that make a person productive, including thinking and reasoning style, behavioral traits, and occupational interests.

  • The personalized description and success strategies assessment (referred to as the PPSS) identifies one's profile pattern and behavioral qualities. This uses the DISC model (dominance, influence, steadiness, and conscientiousness) and can help in your action plan.

Whether you use these assessments or others (some of which are online, some of which are presented in books), you'll be gathering very useful information. In the outer-inner Action Items, you'll see how best to put all this information together and tap into it. For more information, see www.findingrightwork.com.

UNDERSTANDING NETWORKING—PART I

The network you create will be one of the most important resources in your search for right work. As a final part of this set of Action Items, you should begin familiarizing yourself with the vast electronic networking possibilities available today. But let me emphasize: this is just the learning stage. Before you start networking actively, you need to delve deeply into the inner work and have a better idea of what areas you want to explore so you can know what help it is you are asking for. For now, what you want to do is research.

> Begin identifying the people you will include in your FRW (Finding Right Work) network.

> Set aside part of your notebook or your computer files for contact information for your network.

- Right now your network includes people you already know and can comfortably call on, such as
  - family members,
  - friends,
  - personal interest groups,
  - social networks, and
  - business or academic colleagues or fellow alumni.
- At a certain point, you'll include the expanded network of people you are meeting through your project of finding right work.
- Soon enough, you'll find your network growing organically on a constant basis. Once you have a strong sense of the direction of your right work, you'll find it easier and easier to talk with a wide variety of people about it. You'll also find that almost everyone is happy to engage with you. People love to offer help.

> Be alert to the different ways that are available for you to network across many levels. For now, just familiarize yourself with networking opportunities and how they're used.

- In person or in real time. Real time contacts are key. You will meet people every day and strike up conversations with them. As you reach the point that you're ready to go public with the fact that you're researching right work (and after you've done the inner work), you'll want to have business cards so you can exchange information freely. You can make a small batch of them now, and make revised ones later. For now, include the following items on the cards:

- ○ Name, contact information, even a mini photo.
- ○ Something to help others remember you and your search. Make sure it's memorable and represents you well. I've known people who added the initials FRW after their names. They provided an explanation in person and at the bottom of the card. FRW = Finding Right Work.

  Just as your statement of intention will evolve over time, these cards will too. Once you're sure of your area of search, modify your card. Fortunately, business cards are free to inexpensive these days. Just check the Web.

- Facebook. You may already be on Facebook. Even if you like to think that only your friends see it, your contacts for finding your future right work could well be somewhere in that network. Now is the time to make sure your Facebook page is a place anyone could visit and you would be comfortable. Employers are asking for candidate's Facebook passwords. I had a candidate who sabotaged a fabulous job opportunity by not removing a compromising picture posted long ago on a social networking site. Your public image counts. Don't give future contacts and employers a reason to screen you out before you've even met them.

- LinkedIn. As of this writing, LinkedIn is among one of the most vast and valuable networking options for business and professional contacts yet created on earth. Educate yourself on how LinkedIn works and commit to using it at its fullest. If you already are on LinkedIn, be sure your profile is robust and includes a good professional picture. Again, your public image counts. You'll find more on LinkedIn in the third set of Action Items, outer-inner. For that, and other aspects of networking, you'll want to wait until you've done the inner work—and know the parameters of your right work. With that knowledge you can then present your background with clarity and self awareness and in a way that is customized to your priorities and values.

You've taken care of the outer Action Items. But until you're clear about your values and strengths, as well as your priorities relative to work, you're still at the research stage. If, however, you've already realized—and without a doubt—what your right work is, you may find that you can jump to the outer-inner Action Items. Unless you're absolutely certain, take the time now to move to the inner Action Items.

2

Take Time for Reflection

Inner Action Items

Now that you've undertaken some of the beginning Action Items and begun gathering input from external sources and from important people in your life, it's time to go within and begin to reflect on your past as well as your present situation. It's time to begin to listen to your inner voice, your own heart and intuition. It's time to begin to realize that it is in your power to find what work is right for you now; that it is within your power to create a life you love. The effort you put into the inner Action Items now, the time you devote to authentic self-reflection as you begin to really know what is important to you and who you really are, is critical practice for successfully identifying the parameters of your right work.

As part of his commencement address to Stanford University's graduating class back in 2005, Steven Jobs said this: "Your time is limited, so don't waste it living someone else's life. Don't be trapped by dogma—which is living with the results of other people's thinking. Don't let the noise of others' opinions drown out your own inner voice. And most important, have the courage to follow your heart and intuition. They somehow already know what you truly want to become. Everything else is secondary." As Jobs closed his talk, he reminisced about the *Whole Earth Catalog*, which had been a print icon of his generation in the sixties. Launched by Stewart Brand, the *Whole Earth Catalog* was a sort of generational bible of the time, a kind of Google in print for all resources imaginable in life. Jobs ended his speech to the Stanford graduates with the words that were printed on the back cover of the catalog's final edition: "Stay hungry, stay foolish!" Jobs, who died in 2011, seems to have lived by his advice, sage advice that could benefit us all.

3-4-5

PREPARE FOR THE INNER JOURNEY

Now, give yourself permission to believe that you will discover and find your right work. Understand that this permission is always renewable—and that you will likely continue to renew it yourself throughout life. Any time you begin to doubt that it's possible to find your right work, remind yourself that you have already given yourself permission, and you are now on your way, by taking one step at a time.

> ➢ You've heard it said that life is a journey. It's also true that determining and creating your right work is a journey, and—just like your life—it's your journey. Many people don't realize that they only need to remember how to dream again, they only need to hear their inner voices again. If you need a visual cue, just picture Walt Disney's cartoon character, Mickey Mouse, who often piped up with the encouraging words, "If you can dream it, you can do it!"

> ➢ Get to know yourself from the inside-out before trying to define or actively search for your right work. You may be very surprised at how quickly your right work will appear, once you begin to really connect with your authentic self.

ESTABLISH A TIMELINE

Naturally, how long it will take you to determine and find or create your right work depends on a range of factors. In the outer Action Items, in the section on evaluating your current employment status, you began evaluating your current income stream or financial cushion as a first step in financing the project of finding right work. In those Action Items, we kept to the practical side.

Here it's time to get a little deeper into the timeline and examine some questions that may involve facing your inner fears—and not just the kind that pertain to having enough money to live reasonably comfortably while you are on this journey to right work. Depending upon your finances and your emotional comfort level, you may feel the need to set a timeframe or at least a time range for this journey. Perhaps you work more efficiently with deadlines ahead of you. Either way, a timeline is critical.

What factors enter in? Some are measurable; others are intangible.

> Financial resources. Look back at the questions in the outer Action Items and take another look at all your sources of income:
>   - current income,
>   - savings,
>   - any severance pay, and
>   - possibilities for supplementing your income with a temporary or consulting job, even if it's unrelated to your goals.

> Consider how you might save on your current expenses in order to stretch your income during your journey to right work.

> Your current level of self-awareness and clarity about your own priorities, values, talents, and skills as well as your depth of faith in the process and confidence in your ability to find right work will all influence the "rightness" of the work you find and the time it takes you to find it.
>   - Have you recently experienced the reinforcement of great satisfaction in a project or task, whether in your work, as a volunteer, or completely outside of work? That's great news, for that glow will motivate you to search for more opportunities for satisfaction and fulfillment in work.
>   - Conversely, are you frustrated, thwarted, or routinely in pain (physical or emotional) with your work? That's also good news of a sort, for you now know what is wrong work for you. It also means that you are more likely to commit to the time needed to undertake the project of finding your right work. The pain of the present often helps people overcome inertia and the fundamental fear of the future.
>   - If you are only mildly dissatisfied with your work, you may need to dig deeper to give yourself permission to reach for more. Whether that means reaching to expand your expertise, your responsibility, and your satisfaction in your present work or stepping out of your comfort zone into something entirely new is for you to discover.
>   - If you believe that you are lucky to have a job at all, particularly in a difficult economy, with the constant media focus on unemployment rates, your drive and therefore the energy you are likely to

devote to determining your right work may be considerably lower. But don't be lulled into fear-based inertia. The cosmic echo of unfulfilled lives is one of the saddest sounds on the planet. If you are not fulfilling your own life's purpose, if you are not contributing what is possible from your natural talents and abilities, if you are not really in your right work, it will inevitably take a toll on your performance at your current work, in your health and your life, and most of all, in the quality of your contribution to the rest of us. This is your life's journey; it is your time to decide to live your life from the fullness of being in your right work. If you're willing to make the effort, you will find that there is always more out there, as my friend Dick Buxton explains so well in his story of the oasis (at the end of chapter 1).

- If you are comfortable in your job or work, and grateful for just a regular paycheck or predictable income, you may be less motivated to rock the boat. If you are deriving satisfaction in other parts of your life, you may not feel the need to change things. But if the image of those who wait for retirement to pursue their own dreams (and often run out of time in the process) strikes fear in your heart, you'll get moving on it now.
- Spend some time thinking about what has—up until now—kept you from pursuing your right work.
  - List those fears or reasons (some might call them blocks or excuses) and any additional factors that may be in play for you.
  - If you have trouble identifying your own issues, try thinking of individuals you know who are, in your opinion, holding onto jobs that don't satisfy them, match their priorities in life, or use their skills in any meaningful way.
    » Anything seem similar in their lives?
    » Anything familiar that you recognize in yours?

What will be your timeline for finding right work? If I could answer that, I could make a living in prophecy and fortune telling! There is absolutely no way to know. Pick a timeline that is comfortable for you. Vicki Willock (chapter 2) had the luxury of one year. Another client of mine, John Racanelli (who contributed this book's foreword), squeezed in coaching sessions with me even when he was working twelve-hour days. We met at day's end or over coffee whenever possible.

> ➤ I often recommend taking a break from looking for specific answers or for a job for at least thirty to ninety days.
> ➤ Not surprisingly, I've found that people who are able to practice focused self-reflection so as to identify their parameters for right work predictably get results much more quickly than those who have to fit the finding right work project into the corners of their lives. Please know, however, that the number of hours devoted is often less important than the strength of commitment and faith in an outcome that supports your project of finding right work.
> ➤ Many people maintain their current work as they devote part time to determine their new right work.
> ➤ Some people discover that their current work supports top life priorities in such a significant way that, for the present, their right work exists exactly where they are already working. With increased appreciation for strong support of current priorities (making enough money for college tuition, working close to home while they have young children, or working with a stellar mentor) and a change in their own awareness and attitude, they may recognize how they can grow their contribution and talents in their current work, and go about reshaping it more effectively into their current right work.
> ➤ Some choose to dual track, developing their right work as a sideline for a year or two before deciding they can give up their day job. Dual tracking, particularly in a position that pays well without depleting all of your energy, can give you the financial breathing room for your project of finding right work.
> ➤ Some people dual track in a different way, as I have, by cutting back on expenses and lowering overhead or reducing hours needed to work, thus creating more time and resources to develop their right work.

> ➤ There is no way of predicting how long your journey will take. It can be immediate, it can be a month; it can be a year. Even if it's more, the time in self-reflection, planning for and reaching clarity about right work is infinitely more productive and satisfying than many years living a life that isn't the most you can live. As Dick Buxton might say, why linger at a meager oasis when you know you can find a better one? Or, as my Grandma Edie often reminded me, "When you pray, move your feet."

The search business can be very intense. In fact, there have been long stretches in which my business required so much of my time that it nearly overpowered my intention to write this book. The demands of search are immediate and I often allowed that work to press upon the time I had reserved for writing. Even if the hours were still available on my calendar, search demands often trumped my desire to sit down to write.

I began to get frustrated and resentful—so much that I even entertained the idea of leaving my long-term search career to strike out in a completely new direction. After thoughtful reflection, I realized that my search business had always utilized my strongest skills and talents, and that it fully supported my life priorities, strengths and values. But I needed to make room in my life for the book.

My answer was to move my search business out of expensive office space, pare down highly paid staff, and set up my much leaner business in a separate floor of my floating home. These changes allowed me to have the money and time to write while still maintaining a robust recruiting and search practice. My former right work functioned as current right work and supported my growing interest in my newly emerging right work of coaching and writing about right work.

PREPARING YOUR MIND—PART I

Since you have been reading *Finding Right Work* and practicing the Action Items, have you heard voices of doubt? Have you wondered what on earth you're doing, even thinking you can find your own right work? You may need some mental housekeeping and practice to replace those negative voices that often seem to take over.

First, let's focus on ways in which the outside world contributes to the noise in your head. You need to identify this noise, dial this noise down, sometimes way down, so you can manage your thinking. You then will be able to hear your true inner voice and move forward.

➢ Our minds have been programmed—by our parents, our culture, our teachers, the media, and our peers—to think in a certain way. By giving yourself permission to read this book and undertake the Action Items, you've already taken steps to change your life as you learn to manage your own mind, reprogram it in a more positive way, and release your innate potential.

➢ Now it's time to take further steps to actively decrease those outside negative influences that might color what you believe is possible. Those influences creep in from the world at large, from media, and from your friends, family, coworkers, and acquaintances. Start by eliminating negative influences from each category—overall environment, media, and people—and see how your energy rises. Then cut back some more. In this 24/7 wired world, it may seem hard to carve out even a few hours of quiet time, but the rewards are enormous, as you'll soon see.

- Overall environment
  - Spend time outdoors, in nature if possible, alone and without input from electronics. Part of the goal is to be quiet and to actually hear the sounds of nature and, eventually, your own inner voice. That's almost impossible to do, if you are constantly plugged into external noises.
  - Stay fit! Whatever your physical workout routine, whether you're walking, or running, or swimming, or working out, or

161

practicing yoga, do it consistently and treat it as a nonnegotiable commitment.

- ○ Stay present. Diminish multitasking. Focus on your breathing. If your mind wanders, bring it back to the present by noticing your breath. Don't worry about the future, don't obsess about the past. Stay present. Leave your mind alone.

- ○ Stop trying to conduct a meeting from your cell phone while you're running at the gym and watching the bank of TVs, all with crawls across the bottom.

- Media. Going on a media diet can have instant impact and effects. You don't need to retreat into the woods for your own version of Thoreau's Walden Pond experience, but do take a few steps in that direction as an experiment. Spend time at home without external noise coming in from constant music, television, or other electronics.

  - ○ Music? People often gasp at this one. I'm not advocating banning music. Far from it. But the reality is that in our culture, we rarely get any quiet time at all, and even getting solitude in our homes is rare. It is in stillness that our connection to ourselves is rebooted and the opportunity to hear our own inner voice is restored.

  - ○ Television? Minimize your television viewing, especially fear-based and negative shows and newscasts about rampant unemployment and end-of-the-world, fear-driven doom and gloom. Skip the TV news with its emotionalism. Instead, receive your news via the newspaper or customize it from the Internet. Reading about events in the news doesn't trigger the same visceral reaction as emotional commentary and repetitive film footage can. When you read the news, you have more control and picture it in way that's less fear provoking than newscasts (or even radio), both of which embellish everything with emotionalism and high drama.

    - » Unconvinced? Even a very young child can read a bedtime story—think of Maurice Sendak's *Where the Wild Things*

Are—and go right to sleep. But watch the movie version and sleep won't come for hours: the strong images and sound effects spark an entirely different reaction.

» Similarly, do you think you're immune to the impact of external emotionalism? Very few of us are. And if you're beginning a search for a new life, do you really benefit at all from the fearful and hopeless negativity of the news?

» Additional benefits are that reading the news is significantly more time efficient than watching newscasts and won't slow down your brainwaves and deplete your positive energy.

- People with whom you interact. If you've begun talking about your intention to find your right work, be careful to interact with those who are positive and supportive of your journey.

  - Well-intentioned friends and family may ask how your search is going before you have anything to tell them. If you're not yet far enough along that you are ready to discuss it, let them know that you will share information with them when you know more.

  - If questions come from people you've asked for input (per the gathering information section of the outer Action Items), be sure to let them know you want to talk about it—and set up a time and place that is comfortable for both of you.

  - Keep your distance from people who look on the dark side, as did Eeyore, the always-gloomy donkey in the Winnie the Pooh stories.

  - Spend time with other people who respect your journey.

  - Don't share the project or the process of finding right work until you have strength and conviction in what it is you are doing. This will come as you make progress and have significant insights.

- Learn to watch your own mind and deflect anxious and counterproductive negative thoughts by not following them. If you don't follow them, they will disappear.

➢ Stay present to the lessons of this subsection of the Action Items. By controlling your environment and decreasing the negativity that comes in through the media, other people, and old habits of not believing you deserve or could ever find happiness in work, you'll greatly decrease any tendency to sabotage yourself with negative thought habits from the past or worry about the future. In the Action Items coming up, you'll engage in practicing mental fitness so that you can decrease any negativity that you generate in your mind, whether through old fears or new negative influences. The next action item will help you on both counts, learning to observe the external and the internal.

In chapter 5 and in the epilogue you read of how, by listening to my inner voice, I was guided to both my first apartment in San Francisco and my subsequent apartment when my daughter was approaching school age. Both apartments were ideally suited for us in every way. In the Action Items for outer and inner together, you'll read of my search for my next home in a later stage of my life and how the ideal home for me—certainly a tiny needle in a big haystack—appeared right on time.

In all cases, the apartments and homes I have found exactly mirrored my specific priorities and needs of the time. And, in all cases, had I listened to the skeptics and the naysayers, had I not been crystal clear about what I needed, had I not believed it possible, I would never have found my next place. How did I do it? As you'll read, much of it had to do with some techniques that I was learning and that are laced throughout the Action Items. It's all about observing and training your mind (it's a mental fitness practice, remember) to diminish the impact of any negative thinking, envisioning what you want with clarity and openness, and being ready to recognize the right opportunity when it arises.

What I have learned, over and over again, and know, without a shadow of a doubt, is that if you have clarity about what you need and want, truly believe that it is possible to find it, and remain open about the outcome, you will find it or it will find you! This is true with right work and it is true with homes and love partners and parking places and the perfect pair of shoes. It is true with anything and everything needed in life.

PREPARING YOUR MIND—PART II

Now is the time to take a short break and practice observing your mind with a very simple meditation. If you are not familiar with meditation, know that there are many websites and even phone apps that can provide the basics.

A calm abiding meditation, called *shamatha* in Sanskrit, is a very effective and simple method that enables one to calm the mind through observing the mind. It requires only a few simple steps:

> - Relax your body and sit comfortably.
> - Either close your eyes or lower your eyelids so that your gaze rests gently on the floor in front of you.
>   - Observe your breath.
>   - Observe the exhale.
>   - Observe the inhale.
>   - Observe the second at which the inhale becomes the exhale.
> - When thoughts come (as they will) don't follow them. Instead, bring your mind back to your breath and stay present.

The most important step needed to stay present?

> - Don't allow your thought to follow its next connected thought.

Anyone who has started a meditation practice knows that it is easier said than done, particularly in the beginning. But simply watching the breath and observing the mind through meditation provides a calming effect. By focusing on your breath and not following thoughts, you will find your thoughts slowing down . . . moment by moment. As your thoughts slow down, you will experience an increased sense of calmness and peace of mind. One of my teachers likens it to simply letting a glass of fresh orange juice sit undisturbed; very soon, your thoughts settle down, much as the orange pulp naturally sinks to the bottom of the glass.

In addition to a specific time for meditation, you can easily work mini meditations into your daily life, simply by using certain events as prompts.

- ➤ Stuck in traffic? Practice shifting your focus from the traffic to your breath.
- ➤ In line at the grocery? Notice your breathing rather than the long line in front of you.
- ➤ How about watching the exhale of breath as you come to a complete stop at every Stop sign or a red light?
- ➤ You can even take a breath or two before picking up the telephone when it rings. Being present is a gift to the caller.

REFLECT AND PREPARE

Now that you've had an interlude of quiet time, you may well recognize the value you gain when you have learned how to create peace at different times during the day. That's important, because much of what is ahead involves a practice of increasing time for self-reflection and awareness. This quiet time needn't be all at once, or even in large extended periods. The goal is to begin to be aware of your mind enough so that you can direct it rather than have it direct you. Small segments of time will work, once you are in the habit of being in charge of your mind. If you're already intentionally cutting back on the amount of time you spend listening to media and plugged in to your smart phone, finding this time and doing this work will be easier and more productive.

As you focus more on discovering your values, priorities, and talents relative to defining right work, I'll invite you to write a brief career autobiography and a personal mission statement as a way to identify your skills and talents, priorities and values. This reflection is a precursor to that process.

> ➢ Remember the outer Action Items in which you thought about and made lists of projects you've enjoyed, careers you've considered, activities you've dreamed of and imagined yourself doing more often? Now, in some of your quiet time, think more about those experiences and wishes and expand on what you've already written. In doing this, you are increasing your self-awareness and self-knowledge.

> ➢ You've also asked others about their perceptions of who you really are. Review those responses as they come in.

> ➢ Take another look at the information you have and gather still more, bit by bit. Pay careful attention to all information that comes to you. Much of it will be relevant to your self-discovery.
>
>   • Review the information you gathered earlier.
>
>   • Were you truly inclusive? One goal is to gather information about much more than your most recent work experiences. Expand your reach well past work, and much earlier than adulthood. If you haven't already, go all the way back to your childhood. That effort will help you get the most clarity as you look to your future.
>
>   • Allow yourself the time for consistent and focused reflection so that this is thorough.
>
>   • Pay attention to self talk in your head and feelings that come up as you contemplate this task, even including what you're thinking or feeling if you're postponing writing it.

> ➢ Use the following questions as a guide as you spend time thinking about the experiences you've already listed from your past and present work experience, education, volunteer activities, and hobbies. Answering these questions will help you as you begin to create your future.
>
>   • For each job, project, or client, answer the following questions:
>
>   ○ What reasons or priorities led you to take the job, project, or client?
>
>   » How long did you keep that job, project, or client?
>
>   » What were the biggest reasons or priorities that kept you there?

» Describe why you left the job, project, or client, including any additional reasons you now know existed—and what you did next.

◦ Which of your skills, talents, or abilities did you use most in your primary responsibilities?

» How did those change over time?

» Give examples of early responsibilities and later ones.

◦ What was the biggest challenge of the job itself, and in the organization for you?

◦ What would other team members say was your biggest contribution?

◦ What was your biggest lesson from that work experience?

◦ What do you think your employer or client would say was your most consistent strength in the project or job? Your biggest contribution?

◦ What aspects of the job or project would you love to experience again?

◦ What aspects would you never want to repeat?

◦ Are there any mistakes you made or issues you faced that still churn or nag at you? Write them down.

◦ What are the three most important lessons about yourself that you've carried forward from each of these jobs, projects, clients, and experiences?

- Now think about your lifelong learning, including your years of formal education (you may need to break this down for different types or levels of education) and consider the following questions:

◦ What priorities led you to choose your studies or training?

◦ What functional aspects of your learning did you most enjoy?

◦ What were consistently the biggest challenges for you?

◦ What do you think most of your mentors, teachers, or professors would say were your strengths and strongest subjects?

◦ What areas of your education did you love the most?

- What aspects of your education almost always felt like a waste of time?
- What are the three most significant things you learned about yourself and that you've carried forward from your education?
- For each volunteer activity, answer the following questions:
  - What values and priorities led you to take on your volunteer role?
    - » How long did you stay?
    - » What were the principle values and priorities that kept you there?
    - » If you are no longer volunteering in this position or with this organization, why did you leave?
  - What were your primary responsibilities?
    - » How did those change over time?
    - » Give examples of early responsibilities and later ones.
    - » What was the biggest challenge for you?
    - » What was your biggest contribution?
    - » What was the activity's biggest contribution to you?
  - What do you think other volunteers would say was your biggest strength?
  - What aspects of your role there would you love to experience again?
  - What aspects would you never want to repeat?
  - What's the biggest lesson you've carried forward from your volunteer experience in that organization?
- For each hobby you've listed, answer the following questions:
  - What first drew you to this hobby?
  - What interested you the most about participating in it?
  - How long were you active with it? If it's no longer part of your life, why not?
  - What learnings and skills did you acquire?
  - What aspect of it did you enjoy the most?
  - What was the biggest challenge for you?
  - What aspect of the hobby would you love to experience again?

- ○ What aspect would you never want to repeat?
- ○ What's the biggest lesson you've carried forward from your experience in that hobby?

Now that you've gathered even more information from your past, let that percolate on the back burner as you begin your mental fitness routine for the present.

QUIETING YOUR MIND, DAILY PRACTICE—PART I

You've committed to a great deal of change and uncertainty on this journey to right work. During this process and throughout your life, you'll find that staying present, mentally disciplined, and self-reflective makes all the difference. You will begin to be the primary creator of your of own future as you determine what defines your right work, learn how to find it, and create a life you love.

- ➢ Start a daily practice to get your mind in shape and keep it there. Think of it as a fitness program for your mind. You don't need to join a gym or buy special clothes, shoes, or equipment. And there's no commute.
- ➢ Just like any exercise program, you should start small and expand from there. You already have. Remember the calm abiding meditation a few pages back? It is important to do this daily to quiet your mind so that you have access to your deeper inner wisdom and creativity. Soon the time you reserve for yourself will be a welcome daily respite and habit.
  - Try starting with five to ten minutes in the morning, before your day gets going and five to ten minutes in the evening, before you go to sleep.
  - Aim for a consistent practice, morning and night; each reinforces the other.
  - Create that time and you'll soon discover the benefits and may well want to add more time to your workout.
  - Ideally, eventually you'll have a daily practice of thirty minutes every day, divided between the morning and the evening as your "mental

fitness workout." It's a small investment of time as a route to developing positive thinking and trust.

➢ Specific practice tips. As you're starting out with this practice, the purpose is first learning to observe and then beginning to manage the mind. As you progress, the practice will help you open to your own inner wisdom.

- Focus on staying present. When the mind goes forward (into worrying or anticipating the future) or backward (into regret, remorse, or negativity), bring it back to the present by again watching the breath and staying completely present to the inhale and the exhale. This takes practice. And the practice itself brings benefits. You are training and strengthening your awareness of your mind all the time.

- Tips for beginning your morning practice.
  - Begin your morning practice upon awakening with an easy to remember and short positive statement of intention about the day. One option: "Today I am positive, receptive, and expect the best."
  - Give yourself this quiet time for conscious breathing, allowing yourself time to simply be aware of your thinking. Notice what thoughts come up without any effort from you. This time will enable you to be conscious of thoughts that are part of your past programming and will allow you to begin to direct and then reprogram your mind. You will become more aware that your mind can be working for you rather than being in charge of you. This distinction helps you break away from old habits and beliefs.
  - With practice, you will see that you need not be held hostage by your mind's old habits and negative tendencies. You can then choose what you want to believe and think.
  - Remember, your thoughts grow out of seeds of intention. Focus on creating positive intentions and positive thoughts will grow.
  - Don't expect guidance during your meditation, particularly not as you are first practicing. Instead, you are creating the intention of accessing inner guidance, providing a foundation for informa-

tion and direction that will eventually be available for any aspect of your life.

- o In time, you will begin to carry the awareness and mindfulness of your morning practice into the rest of your day.
- o Remember, whenever you are staying present and observing your own mind, you are in a place of meditation, with opportunity for enhanced access to powerful inner wisdom.

- Tips for beginning your evening practice.
  - o Consider your current nighttime routine. If, for instance, you typically close the day by watching TV or reviewing a list of the next day's activities and to-do items, either move those activities or be sure to give yourself some time afterwards before beginning your evening practice.
  - o As with your morning practice, your evening practice should begin with quieting the mind. Watch your breathing and don't follow thoughts that arise. Allow yourself to observe thoughts without reacting to or following them. Eventually, the thoughts will slow down and the normal bubble machine of your mind will wind down. As you follow your breath, allow yourself to relax.
  - o This evening practice will calm the mind and prepare it for peaceful sleep. You will find yourself getting to sleep more easily and feeling more rested when you awaken.

QUIETING YOUR MIND, DAILY PRACTICE—PART II

Work on developing conscious habits of mind that create and maintain positive expectations and thinking throughout the day. As you begin to self-reflect and observe and train your mind, you will experience some or all of the following.

- ➢ Pay attention and listen. You will find information from a multitude of unexpected resources.
  - • Conversations you may overhear by accident inspire a significant idea or direction.

- Articles arriving via email from friends, posted online, or in print jump out at you and have an important message.
- Book titles suddenly catch your attention and become important signposts for your journey.
- Conversations with people you know or happen to meet are relevant to your process in a significant way.
- Dreams will answer specific questions asked before sleep and offer direction at a specific fork in the road on your journey. Yes, a dream journal is a great idea.

➤ Notice positive, creative, productive thoughts that emerge and focus on them.

- Whatever you pay attention to will expand in its influence on your mind. Listen carefully and follow the creative thoughts without judgment or concern about how things can possibly happen or the "impossibility of it all."
- Write down your thoughts and review them consistently.
- Write down ideas even without knowing where they are taking you.

➤ Begin to allow yourself a level of excitement about the ideas and answers that are beginning to appear.

➤ If your mind is wanting to "know" the specifics of your right work before you know, return the mind to the project of determining priorities, values, talents and skills rather than what exactly will be your right work. Use this statement as a mantra: "Let go of needing to know!" Repeat it often.

- Begin to teach yourself not to focus on or follow regrets about the past or fears about the future that may arrive in your mind. Don't let your mind control you; instead, begin to observe and manage your mind. Acknowledge the existence of negative and fearful thoughts and their tendency to arrive habitually. Don't follow them.
- You can also train the mind back to the present. How? A spiritual mentor of mine teaches that the untrained mind is like an untrained young puppy that is peeing all over the house. What to do? When

you catch the puppy peeing, calmly and gently put it back on the paper of staying present and positive. Do this gently and firmly, again and again. One day, your puppy will be trained.

- Decide not to allow negative thoughts, any follow-up thoughts, or any preprogrammed naysaying habits of mind to have a voice. Keep training your puppy.

- Only a tiny percentage of things that we worry about actually occur. As Deb Wetherby said (back in chapter 4), "Funny enough, when I look back on it, only 5 percent of my fears ever came to pass. Five percent!" Surely that's too small a percentage to be a roadblock on the path to your own right work. Don't spend your time and energy in worry. My definition of worry is that it is embellished and enhanced negative thinking.

- Remember: where you put your attention matters. Whatever you think most about will come to pass. You are what you think. Whatever you focus on gets bigger. Make sure you take charge of your mind and have it focus on the positive expectation of discovering who you really are, especially at the level of your priorities, values, talents and skills.

There's a story of an airline traveler who was comfortably ensconced in her seat, in the beginning of a transatlantic flight. She was flying first class, and well accustomed to good service.

The flight was delayed and she pulled down the tray table in front of her to use her iPad. The tray was dirty. Instead of simply asking for a clean-up, her thoughts rushed to "This airline has really gone downhill. Once, everything was well taken care of. And now the tray is dirty! I wonder what else they're cutting back on. If they don't clean the trays, it must mean that they're cutting back on service. The maintenance crew has also been cut back. Maybe they don't even do maintenance right anymore." Within sixty seconds her mind had morphed her tiny concern into an inevitable plane crash.

The moral? Don't let your equivalent of a dirty tray table intrude. Let a dirty tray table be just a dirty tray table. Just take note of it and move on.

Don't expect to be able to eliminate all negative thoughts once and for all. It's a goal, rarely reached. Do you know why the Buddha is also known as "The Victorious One"? It's said that at the moment right before his own Enlightenment, he had finally, after a lifetime of dedicated intense devotion, study, and practice, vanquished all negative thinking.

> Don't allow yourself to follow the fearful thoughts either. Remember, when you follow a thought, it gains in impact and power and can take all of your motivation and commitment for positive change with it.
> Most fearful thoughts (except perhaps if you are staring at a great white shark while snorkeling) are old habits of mind, old beliefs from our mind's history.
>   • They often relate to thoughts such as not having anything special to offer the world, not having enough money, not deserving to be happy, or the difficulty of finding any work, much less "right" work! "You are lucky to have any job at all!" is a thought that is prevalent in a changing economy, as is "There are no jobs out there!"
>   • Imagine you've told someone that the work you're now doing isn't really making you happy and you're taking steps to discover what truly is your right work. Imagine that the person's response is along the lines of, "Why do you think work is called 'work?' Life is difficult! What do you think, that life is one breathless moment after another?" Instead of automatically being discouraged, you can calmly respond from your trained, calm, centered mind. You might say something like "I believe that when people are in their right work

they are able to give more of themselves to the world. And yes, they are happier."

- Negative and fearful thoughts are preprogrammed by families, teachers, the beliefs and paradigms of the present culture as well as old defensive mind patterns from past experience. The good news is that habits and beliefs can be changed. As my Tibetan Buddhist teacher Lama Orgyen Chowang Rinpoche explains, the mind is like an old record with deep grooves of mind habits. The deeper the groove, the more easily the mind goes to that groove or thought. These grooves can be sanded down with a conscious focus on positive new beliefs and thoughts. With more and more positive thought, negative and fearful habits of mind will be diminished. Thought by positive thought, you will shift your mind from impossibility to possibility thinking. Your positive thinking creates new, previously unimagined possibilities.

Observing and training your mind is a lifelong commitment. For all of us, it's an ongoing practice. (Come to think of it, so is exercise: you can't get in great shape with a short effort and expect to stay that way unless you commit to ongoing exercise and healthy diet.) To learn to manage your own mind and successfully replace old habits of fear or negativity, you will want to increase your self-reflection time and learn to be in close charge of your own mind. Every minute of every day offers new opportunities for increased mental fitness. Every bit of that fitness strengthens your connection with your inner wisdom, guidance, and self-awareness. Increased self-awareness always inspires increased self-confidence.

Mind your mind. You can learn to select and observe your thoughts and, as much as possible, choose not to follow negative thoughts. If your self talk is negative, you can learn to change the channel: you can exorcise those gloom and doom tracks from your head, moment by moment. You can change the channels of your mind.

Commit to an ongoing mental fitness practice to create a positive mindset on a daily basis. By establishing these practices as embedded habits, you'll find yourself connecting more and more easily with who you really are. As your access to inner wisdom increases, the guidance available to you will grow. The more guidance you have, the more clarity you have. The more clarity you have, the closer you are to finding right work and creating a life you love.

In the next set of Action Items, you'll take major steps forward as you weave your observations from your work in the outer Action Items and the inner Action Items together.

3

Identify and Find Your Right Work

Outer and Inner Action Items, Together

Now that you've taken the basic steps of learning more about yourself, observing and learning to manage your mind, increasing your mental fitness, and tapping into your own inner wisdom, it's time to combine your outer and inner work and take your practice to another level. In working on the Action Items of this section, you'll use your growing clarity about your strongest talents and abilities, along with your awareness of your values and highest current priorities to develop a brief career autobiography and mission statement. These next steps build upon the self-knowledge you've gleaned in the process, and will guide and direct you as you begin to identify, create and find your right work. You'll also develop an expanded self-aware-ness and clarity about your relationship to work itself: why you have made decisions to leave work or accept work in the past. You will begin to see the general parameters of what has been your previous work. You will then be-gin to expand your personal and professional network and learn to use tools that will move you closer and closer to identifying real opportunities that reflect the work that is right for you now.

MINING YOUR PAST, CREATING YOUR FUTURE—PART I

In the chapters, you read of people reviewing their lives by drafting their career autobiographies. At the end of chapter 4, you read the directions that we provide to potential candidates in my search business. The discussion that follows expands on this framework, to help ensure that you make a thorough evaluation of yourself as you determine your own right work.

By now, you've already gathered much of the material you need for writing your career autobiography and personal mission statement. In my experience, most people find great value in these exercises since they rarely give themselves the time to stop long enough in life to assess the past or to create the future, particularly through the perspective of an assessment or review. Surprises and Aha! moments often emerge. This work will offer invaluable insights for your process as you progress along the journey. Enjoy it!

- ➤ In the outer Action Items and the inner Action Items, you've written down memories from your childhood on up and reflected on that information. Now, as you prepare to write this career autobiography, you'll review those facts and findings, and integrate them into current relevant information about yourself.
- ➤ What is it?
  - This is a brief work-related autobiographical sketch (perhaps two to three pages) for your own use.
  - It's not a full-blown autobiography, but a tight recap, focusing on your work as it relates to what you have done in the past and why.
- ➤ What's the purpose?
  - It's simply another way in, to help you further clarify your skills and talents, priorities and values. The more you know yourself at this level, the closer you are to identifying your right work.
  - Taking the time to make the exercise accurate and authentic will help ensure that you become genuinely aware and appreciative of your talents and strengths, priorities and values, whether it's as a base for your own self-knowledge, setting up your LinkedIn profile, in your revised statement of intention, preparing your résumé, or beginning to have more clarity about what work is right for you now.
  - Even if you're currently in search of an interim position to help finance a longer-term search for right work, your efforts on the autobiography now will be critically important for relevant information as you move forward.
- ➤ Reviewing the facts and findings for your career autobiography. In reviewing the essence of the work projects and experiences over your life to this point, take time for the following steps:

- Identify work that used your gifts—your strongest skills, talents, and abilities.
  - From your perspective.
  - From any outside assessments, both those from people you've asked (previous supervisors, close friends, spouse, children) and any professional assessments you've had done.
- Be aware of what stories consistently arise in your mind about yourself and about how you believe the world always works. Pay attention and write down what comes to mind. Be sure to include the following:
  - Old negative mindsets or beliefs that are the loudest and most persistent.
  - New information, new positive directions or ideas of possibility that inspire you and support you.
  - Any new interests or passions that you realize are present and perhaps you hadn't considered possible as work. Consider
    - » people you admire,
    - » subjects that you're drawn to or that spark passions,
    - » help you would love to give, and
    - » organizations you find compelling.
  - Areas of little or no interest to you, even areas that you realize you find tedious or that actually repel you, which might be
    - » types of people or behaviors,
    - » industries you are not drawn to or don't respect or align with,
    - » styles of working or being, or
    - » work you find meaningless for any reason.
- For each point you've included in your list, ask these questions:
  - Were you really engaged, and happy? Trust your gut.
  - Did any negatives appear? There may be some that you listed in working through the inner Action Items and some that occur to you now. Any mistakes and issues that you remember may be your clue to values disparity in the workplace.

» Draw on your mental fitness practice to help provide distance from your thoughts so that you can observe these negative stories and learn from them without getting drawn into worry or fear. Again, don't follow your thoughts into either the future or the past. Be aware that the present has no meaning other than what you decide to place on it. Remember that as you are changing your mind, you are changing your life experience.

~ Observing these negatives will actually help you determine where you should not be headed, sort of a reverse signpost.

~ Knowing the negatives will help you know yourself better so you won't do the same thing over and over again, expecting different results. You will avoid repeating history and be able to support your weakness, whether by learning new skills or teaming up with someone who is strong in places where you are not.

- Continue to research what you don't yet know, to gather new and pertinent information and begin to learn to listen to your inner voice for guidance and direction as often as possible.

DRAFTING YOUR CAREER AUTOBIOGRAPHY

As you review your notes and focus on the positive experiences in your education and your career, you'll find your strengths in front of you.

➢ Identify what you know are your strongest talents and strengths and list them. Be sure to look across all categories: work, education, volunteer activities, hobbies. Capture all of your strengths across all endeavors. Be inclusive.

➢ Be sure you've covered everything that you need. Double check your list against the information that has come in from others and from any professional assessments.

➤ Weave your strengths and talents into the narrative description that connects highlights from your life and work, including development of your skills and talents.

➤ In drafting your autobiography, be sure it includes a statement of values and purpose separate from your priorities and acknowledges any prevailing passions relative to work.

➤ The link between your work history and your priorities and values is not always apparent until you take time for reflection and specific focus. On a general level, the skills and abilities you love to use will also generally reflect a lifelong pattern that probably began when you were a child and strengthened as time went on.

MINING YOUR PAST, CREATING YOUR FUTURE—PART II

Now's the time to review your career autobiography to identify the recurrence of strongest talents, reflected values, and an awareness of past priorities relative to work.

➤ Analyzing and using your autobiographical information. Identify the wisdom of your autobiography and other information about yourself and celebrate your talents and strengths as you fully accept your weaknesses. All of this is critical to discovering your right work.

- Focusing on values and priorities.
  - ○ Based on what you know about yourself and the information in your career autobiography, identify your top life values and five strongest priorities relative to work. Remember, as discussed in chapter 4, your values are the foundation; your priorities change over time, depending on your age and stage.
  - ○ What are your most important beliefs or values? A value is a guiding principle—perhaps a strong work ethic, honoring and caring for family, compassion, service to others, the importance of education—that is the foundation of how you live your life. Your values often determine why you make certain important decisions.

- » Some people make a long list and then distill it by considering this question: What five values are nonnegotiable for you?
- » Another question that works: What values do you most want to transmit to your children?
- » If you have trouble determining your values, write what you're sure of and make a list of values you admire in others.
- What are your top priorities relative to your work? Priorities change throughout life. They may include financial compensation, meaningfulness of the work itself, proximity to home, family, work/life balance, amount of time required, industries in which you could not work (some people cannot work for tobacco companies or companies that make weapons) and anything else that you know is important relative to your work at this stage in life.
  - » List as many as you can think of, and at least five to ten.
  - » Review your list and see if your priorities give more insight into your values. If, for instance, the priorities you've listed have to do with providing for your children, then family clearly belongs on your value list right now.

    As a personal example, when I was raising my daughter as a single mom, all of my priorities—flexible hours, good income, working near home—were clearly centered on the value of family life. Over time, and as my daughter's needs changed, my priorities changed. Even so, they continue to rest on unchangeable values. The value of family life remains right up there and is now reflected by my involvement with my grown daughter, her husband, and her young family. The value of service to others is an increasing part of my life, in my search work, my coaching, and in writing this book. Making time for spiritual practice and for exercise remain priorities throughout.

Among the questions we pose to candidates is one asking them to describe their top five priorities relative to their current search for work. Here's what one candidate wrote in her initial list of priorities when she came to me in her job search.

My top five priorities relative to work right now are to

1. strengthen and use my strong technical and project management skills with a growing company,
2. maintain work/life balance,
3. earn a base salary of at least $70,000 a year,
4. work for a company that is contributing something good to the world, and
5. be able to take public transportation to work.

This was a good start, and I thought it important that she take steps to be clear about the link between her priorities and values. So I used a variation of my magic wand question and said, "I'd like you to pretend again that anything is possible, and write down two more priorities relative to work. Remember that you have a magic wand, money is no object, and success is guaranteed."

The magic wand question doesn't provide a breakthrough moment for everyone (as it did for Linda Wosskow in chapter 2), but often it does spark an incremental shift. Keeping the process open and believing you can have it all counts for a lot.

When she came up with her two additional priorities—

6. have Tuesday evenings and Saturday mornings free for the yoga class that I like to teach, and
7. continue to have time for my volunteer work at the homeless shelter in San Francisco.

I had a much better sense of what was important to her and what positions could use her skills. I knew that a 24/7 job that would demand erratic and long hours wouldn't serve her for the long term. With that additional information, I was getting closer to learning what her true priorities were.

Too often, people limit themselves in their priority list since they don't realize that by being very specific and expanding their list to include what's really important to them, they multiply the probability of their connection with right work.

> Clarify your values list so that it reflects those principles that inspire and guide your life.
> Incorporate all of your values and priorities in easy-to-remember affirmations. If, for example, one of your priorities is to be financially independent and have more free time, your affirmation might be: "I experience an abundance of both money and time in my life."
> As often as possible, take note of thoughts and feelings that are recurring. Discipline yourself to not follow negative thoughts and to nurture possibility and positive thoughts.
>   • If negative thoughts reoccur, have an affirmation at the top of mind and replace the negative thought with a positive one ("I experience lavish, unfailing abundance.") that you can repeat until the negative thought has disappeared.
>   • Repeat the positive outcome and experience you want to reinforce over and over again.
>   • Begin to believe that you do have a magic wand, that money is no object, and that success is guaranteed!
> Again, without allowing your mind to fall back into a negative spiral, take note of what attracts you and what repels you. Both hold important clues.

Throughout the economic downturn, when so many people were laid off, I saw that many of those who got the "cosmic boot" from big corporations were kicked out of work they had actually outgrown. The good news is that a high percentage of those people who are let go from corporate jobs end up creating work in consulting or find jobs that are far more closely attuned to their current life priorities and to their unique gifts and talents. Some of them have felt as though they were released from a kind of work life to which they could never again return. More than a few laid off employees have wound up with consulting or contract work from their former employers and done quite well in the process.

When Robert Mondavi's cosmic kick came along, he took the time to identify his strengths and weaknesses and to evaluate and refocus his passions. That "leave of absence" from the family wine business became the defining moment of renewal and career rebirth for him. Marnie Walker hadn't yet considered what her life's work would be when, in high school, she was faced with a life-threatening illness that gave her the time and need for introspection and a serious evaluation of who she really was at a very young age.

For both of these people (discussed in chapter 3) and so many more, this self-reflection and self-awareness empowered them, propelling them toward new right work and giving them the guidance to create and find what, at the outset and from the outside, was unknown.

As Dick Buxton (also chapter 3) might say, these changes and evaluations pushed them to move on, to find the next oasis, the one that was right for them at that moment in time.

- ➢ Focusing on strengths, talents, and skills.
  - • Based on your career autobiography, identify your strengths, talents, and skills relative to work.
    - ○ List these strengths, talents, and skills. Be sure to highlight any that you feel are your strongest talents, perhaps those that you most love to use in your work and in your life.

- ○ Set the three strongest up as affirmations. If, for example, one of your strongest talents is relating quickly and effectively with other people, your affirmation might be "I connect easily and effectively with many people as I contribute to work I love."
- ○ Periodically review your list and update it with any newly discovered skills, talents, strengths, and priorities.
- ○ Also, look at this list in light of finding a need in the world and filling it with your strengths. Find a need and fill it!

Many years ago, I read a memorable story about a woman who then lived in the public housing projects in Chicago. She was single, had a number of children, and was on welfare. She got tired of seeing and avoiding the dog poop in front of her building and began collecting it. Soon, she was collecting it at neighboring buildings as well. The city heard about her and after a time, asked if they could hire her to clean up all the dog poop around all of the apartments. She hired helpers, started a company, and grew the company. In time, she contracted with a fertilizer company and recycled the poop. She now operates a thriving company in Chicago with dozens of employees, and is off welfare.

Who would have thought there'd be a business in this task? In fact, there was such a need that there are now many companies advertising themselves as dog poop cleanup specialists.

- ➤ Reinforce your self awareness.
  - Make a complete list of your top priorities, values, strengths, talents and skills relative to your right work.
  - Make multiple copies of these lists and post them so you'll be sure to see them many times a day (more is better). Be creative, and use lots of options.

- ○ Hard copies: on the bathroom mirror, on your closet door, by your landline phone, folded in your wallet (even if you don't read it each time you open your wallet, you will see them), on the refrigerator, tucked inside the books you're reading, on your car's dashboard or passenger seat or on the kitchen counter.
- ○ Techno/electronic: as your screensaver on your electronic devices, from your computer and phone to your iPod or iPad.
- ○ If you're dual tracking, you can put these lists (or abbreviated versions that will serve to remind you of them) where only you will see them.
- ○ In time, these lists will become affirmations that are embedded in your memory, further strengthening your determination on the path to right work.

- ➤ Stay present. While you are making, reading, and reviewing these lists, let go of needing to know specifics about what your right work is. Don't obsess about getting the answer. Instead strengthen your confidence that you are moving in the right direction by transforming your angst into an affirmation: "I am more aware of who I really am. For now, I let go of needing to know what my right work is. I know that I will discover and recognize my right work."
- ➤ You're not yet looking around for something specific: you're still clarifying the details of your values, priorities, talents, skills, and gifts and staying open to emerging possibilities.

Why all the lists? The lists function as a script for creating the movie of your life. You are the producer, director, and star of the movie. The more specific you are, the more clarity you have about what you want in your movie, the sooner it will be produced. If you're skeptical about the value of creating and posting these lists, take a moment to read "The Dragon Boat of My Dreams" in the following pages. The more specific your lists (of values, priorities, skills, talents, gifts, desires) the more prepared you are, the more quickly you will recognize the opportunities that are your next right work and the people who can help get you there.

I've included the Dragon Boat story here to encourage you to conduct your own experiment. Purge any old voices that whisper, "Who am I to get everything I want?" Distance yourself from anyone who shouts a similarly negative idea to you. Instead, realize that if you are in your right work it will benefit others as well as you. You are unique. You have talents to contribute that no one else can give exactly as you can!

The Dragon Boat of My Dreams

In some ways, one kernel for this book began with a personal crisis many years ago. I was then living on Issaquah Dock in Sausalito, California, in a small, beautiful floating home that I had begun renting after a challenging divorce and a significant business loss. The home was a refuge and place of healing for me; I loved it and the supportive, caring people who all made their homes in Richardson Bay on the dock's sixty five houseboats.

One day, my landlady (who was also my coach and friend) told me that she had sold her house on land and wanted to move back to her houseboat. After ten years of renting her floating home, I would have sixty days to find a new home. I could not imagine living anywhere else and I cried for an entire weekend, with a depth of sadness I had rarely experienced.

As my mind and heart began to accept the inevitable change ahead, I decided to transform my sadness and disappointment into anticipating the possibility of living somewhere even more wonderful. The classes that I had been taking in "Science of Mind" at the Center for Spiritual Living were timely. We had been learning how to focus the mind in conscious and clear thinking with directed meditation and focus to manifest specifically what it is that we need and want in our lives. We learned that the mind is the creator of all experience and that focused attention creates desired outcome.

I was not, at that point, entirely sure I could manifest anything at all that I wanted since my personal and professional lives both seemed to have bottomed out, but I decided that I had nothing to lose and would do an experiment of my own. I sat down and made a long and detailed list of what I wanted in my next home. I wrote down everything, including wanting a perfect home on the upper end of the dock where the water was deep enough to have a boat, a home that was large enough to accommodate my business, that was open and light and spacious, that I could afford, and much more. I decided to believe that I could have it all. I gave up trying to figure out how it would happen and when. I concentrated on believing that it would all come true and my only job was to know exactly what I wanted and trust that it would arrive. It was, as you can see, quite a list.

- a floating home in Sausalito
- located on Upper Issaquah dock
- large enough to have my office: workspaces for my assistant and for me
- spacious, light and open feel
- dining room large enough for seated dinner parties up to twelve people
- deep water dock
- power boat
- owner will carry back financing for five years
- furnished
- uncluttered, Asian decor
- spectacular and unobstructed view of the mountain and the bay
- available within one to two months
- down payment required not more than $120,000 (all I had)
- quiet neighbors
- in good condition
- no immediate repairs needed

- peaceful and warm energy
- at least three bedrooms
- at least three bathrooms
- able to keep kayaks on attached dock
- carpeted
- well-lit space
- comfortable for large gatherings
- top of the line appliances
- quality fixtures and accoutrements

I kept that list in front of me morning, noon, and night. I had a copy in my car, on my refrigerator, on the kitchen counter, on the bathroom mirror, in my notebook for work, and propped beside my bed. I even had a huge version on the entryway mirror. The list was the first thing I saw when I woke up and the last thing before I slept. I had decided that, if my experiment was going to be fair to my teacher, I should really pull out all the stops. I made the decision to have everything I wanted in my new home. Absolutely everything. I trained my mind to move away from doubt and into belief. I believed I would find my new home. I wouldn't allow myself to think, even for a moment, that there was any doubt in my mind whatsoever.

I looked at my list all the time; I held it in my hands and in my heart. Several weeks into my experiment, a friend of mine and I headed down the dock on a Sunday, toward some open houses that were for sale at the end of the dock. I had tucked the list inside my purse.

As we were walking toward the open houses, we saw a neighbor heading toward us, one of the few I didn't know personally. His house, the Dragon Boat, was the tallest houseboat in the harbor, had been under constant renovation, and was rumored to be spectacularly beautiful inside. I was surprised that my friend knew the owner. After he introduced us, practically the first thing out of my mouth was, "Wow, you're living in the Dragon Boat! I've heard so much about it. Could we take a tour?" He invited us in.

I walked into the foyer and gasped at the majesty and splendor of the place and the view. I walked slowly into the large living room whose sky-high ceilings were softened with what seemed like miles of beautiful fabric. As I looked around, I saw a marble fireplace and a kitchen with granite counters. I suddenly and surely knew that this house was my house and had everything on my list. I also knew that it wasn't for sale.

I had, however, heard through the dock's powerful grapevine that the owner was thinking of taking a trip around the country in a bus that he called the Dragon Bus. The thought came to me that perhaps he would rent the house to me. I hadn't even seen the rest of the house yet but I knew this was my house; I just needed to figure out how the owner was going to realize that also. I waited a couple of minutes and said, "I heard you were leaving the area. Would you be interested in renting the Dragon Boat?" He quickly told me that he'd already rented it. I walked slowly around the living room again. "Hmmm," I said as I walked to where he was standing. "Wouldn't you rather sell the house?"

The owner didn't wait a second before saying, "Oh, no! I would have no interest at all in selling." In case I hadn't heard, he added, "So, no. The answer is no."

I walked away, looked up at the mezzanine, and asked to see the rest of the house. I walked upstairs to a spectacular master bedroom suite. There were dolphins on the fixtures at the sink and a mermaid etched in glass. The view of Mount Tamalpais was even more spectacular from the fourth story.

I returned downstairs with a deepening conviction that this was indeed, my house: it had everything on my list. I returned to the living room and approached the owner again. "Are you sure you don't want to sell this house?" I asked.

Looking a bit irritated, he replied, "No, Leni, I don't want to sell the Dragon Boat. I just renovated it. I love it here. I don't want to sell it!"

I walked over to the huge living room window, saw water birds resting on the pilings, and approached the owner again. "Come on," I said, "Everybody has a price! What is your price?"

My friend looked at me as though I was absolutely nuts. The owner looked at me in irritated disbelief and then he smiled. "OK," he said, "I'll play. I suppose everybody does have a price. Let's see, if I were going to sell the Dragon Boat to you, I would sell it to you for $730,000."

That number was just about twice what the house was worth at the time. I quickly did some calculations in my head. I had been renting an office for my business and that expense ($3,000 a month) would go away, a certain percentage of the cost of the house would be deductible, and so on. Interesting enough, 20 percent of his number was not a great deal more than I had already collected for a down payment. I waited about two minutes and replied, "That is about twice what the house would sell for. So, if I do buy your house, you'll have to include the furniture since my furniture would never fit here. I'd like you to leave the art that is on the walls since there is so much wall space. Also, you'll have to carry the mortgage for me for five years. I'll give you 20 percent down." I walked out on the deck and came back, adding, "And I would appreciate you leaving the power boat as well."

"But," he practically shouted, "it is not for sale!"

Without missing a beat, I said, "You just told me that if I paid you $730,000 you would sell it to me."

His voice ratcheted down a notch as he asked, "You would pay me $730,000?"

"Yes, I would," I said. "But let's not be hasty. Let's sleep on it and I'll come back tomorrow morning. And if we do this," I said, "I need to move in thirty days from now."

The owner was looking as though he was in a serious state of shock. My friend was looking at me as though he was now sure I was certifiably cuckoo. As the two of us left, the owner asked, "What do we do about Mark, the renter?" I said, "We'll have to give him some consideration money. Let's split that."

As my friend and I walked back down the dock, he exploded with very strong thoughts about my madness. His doubts (which sounded a lot like the old negative voices I hadn't allowed to participate in my experiment) just rolled off of me. I knew that this was the right move for me. It was an intuitive wisdom and strength coming out.

Later that night, I did the numbers. I knew the house would increase in value and that I would stay in the house for a good number of years. The next morning, I gave the owner a check for $145,000 and I moved into the Dragon Boat thirty days later.

This was, for me, proof that we can manifest whatever it is we need or want—if we have faith that it will happen.

My houseboat has been featured on *The Today Show*; it is on HGTV on the show *Overboard* and on the Travel Channel's *Extreme Houseboats*. I've yet to do the research, but it may be the tallest houseboat in the world. It is certainly one of the most beautiful—breathtakingly beautiful!

By the way, many years later, and even in a down economy, the Dragon Boat's monetary value is well above what I paid. The value it has added to my life, my well being, and my business continues to multiply.

Any time I think that maybe the mind doesn't create reality, I gaze around my beautiful home. It's proof enough for me that when you focus on what you want and pay attention, the universe does respond. What will arrive in your life is always more wonderful than your dreams. We all have this power. We just need to realize it, practice it, and use it!

BRING OUTER AND INNER TOGETHER

By now, you are very comfortable with your mental fitness practice. You see that it is providing you with increased positive energy, inner guidance, and clarity. Your practice is strengthening your ability to manage your thoughts and your mind as you sweep away negative thoughts. You are reinforcing positive thoughts and are becoming more and more aware of your strengths, talents, values, and priorities.

- ➤ You are getting better at staying present, and better able to overcome old habits of mind.
- ➤ When negative thoughts intrude, it is getting easier to let them go.
- ➤ Your affirmations are helping you strengthen positive expectations and change your experience.
- ➤ If you haven't already, now is the time to expand your mental fitness practice to an hour a day, divided between your morning and evening workout practices. Add time incrementally until you reach that goal.
  - • This commitment of focused time is a critical component of changing your mind and your life. Being able to change your mind is required to discover what work is right and then to be guided to it.
  - • Until taking time for mental fitness is truly a habit, you will need to physically put this time on your calendar. I sign myself out in my calendar for both meditation and physical exercise. The time has become sacrosanct. I experience a monumental difference in the positive quality of my life when I exercise mentally and physically versus when I don't.
  - • If you find you have trouble scheduling the time for practice each day, build in an affirmation: "I practice observing and training my mind on a daily basis and experience mental fitness increasing every day."
  - • When beginning your mental workout, start by becoming aware of your breathing rather than any other thoughts that may be dominating your mind. Another affirmation may help: "I manage my mind and thoughts as I become more and more connected with who I really am."

195

> ➢ With the additional time in your practice (and your increased skill) you can now add a deeper level to your mental fitness routine.
>   - Before your morning practice, read your list of priorities, values, skills, talents. If you haven't already incorporated some affirmations relative to this step, you might add, "I am in work that is aligned with my values and priorities, uses my talents and skills, and provides me with abundant income."
>   - Night practice is very different from morning practice. At night, focus on that for which you are most grateful. This focus helps reinforce the positive. It will also improve sleep and lead to being more focused on positive expectations and gratitude.
> ➢ Your daily practice will allow you know more and more clearly what your right work is.
> ➢ The broad picture of your right work will emerge from this practice. The more clarity you gain, the more your clarity will lead to specifics, including resources for networking and connecting with the right people and opportunities for relevant work.
> ➢ Your emerging clarity will also help you to say no to work that is not right work for you.

CREATING YOUR FUTURE: WRITING YOUR PERSONAL MISSION STATEMENT

Realize that you do indeed have a magic wand. With that wand and your new clarity of mind, you develop a personal mission statement written in the present tense. This statement incorporates what you know to be your strongest values, talents, and priorities relative to work and then affirms that you are in your right work, using your strengths and reflecting your top priorities relative to work. Your mission statement should be short, easy to remember, and reflect the core of what you know are the parameters of your right work. My mission statement follows:

> By working in step with our highest priorities, natural talents, and values, we increase our happiness and create lives we love. Helping people find the path to working right is my right work.

Now, with all that you've learned, write a draft of your personal mission statement. Don't be surprised if you need to write a few before one rings true.

TAKING IT OUT THERE: FINDING YOUR OWN RIGHT WORK

Once you've identified your priorities, strengths, abilities, and values, and developed your autobiography and mission statement, you are ready for identifying, creating, developing, or finding your own right work. All of what you've learned to this point has prepared you. And, through what you've worked on, you've expanded your network and increased the ways in which right work will appear for you. And now, for further impact,

> ➤ Become the person you dream of being! Commit yourself completely to your project, appoint yourself as the dedicated director, producer, and star of the movie of your own work life. Have absolute faith in the positive outcome of finding your right work.

> ➤ You've done this already, really; you've already taken charge. You've read *Finding Right Work*, you've worked through the outer and the inner action steps, you're working on the outer and inner steps together, you're developing your mental fitness, and you've done a lot of the background research for yourself. In effect, you've already been acting as your own coach and project manager.

> ➤ Now, jump off one more very big cliff and commit to believing, with no room for doubt, in the certainty of identifying and finding the work that is right for you at this moment in time! For that, you need a campaign manager.

BECOME YOUR OWN CAMPAIGN MANAGER—PART I

As the manager of your campaign for developing or finding your own right work, you must advocate for yourself and advertise yourself. Just like the best campaign managers, you must be proactive and resourceful. You must take charge of what you need to learn and discover. You must organize and network. You must stay resilient, dedicated, committed and expecting to win—every minute of every day.

> ➤ Campaign managers are masters of networking, of creatively choreographing opportunities to leave no relevant stone unturned for communication and networking, and of making the best of every occasion as it arises. They always have the mission statement in front of mind.

> ➤ Campaign managers also know the priorities of the campaign and what components are critical to the candidate's success.

> ➤ Great campaign managers are unstoppable. As manager of your own campaign for right work, you need to adapt that unstoppable attitude, resourcefulness, and tenacity as you march forward, even if you sometimes feel tired or discouraged.

> ➤ One important step is to be as specific as possible with the parameters for your script for right work, inside and out.

>> • Inside: What do you want for work structure?
>>> ◦ self-employed or employed
>>> ◦ location of employer or client
>>> ◦ industry, profit or nonprofit
>>> ◦ values of employer or client

>> • Take note of what you are drawn to and be alert for organizations that are aligned.

>> • Outside: How do you find organizations that might fit well? What types of jobs match your current priorities, values, abilities and skills? If the idea of consulting or being self-employed is attractive, what needs can you fill with your experience and skill set? You can do much of this research on the Internet or through your local library. That's your next step.

BECOME YOUR OWN RESEARCHER

In the world of politics, a campaign manager would have the big picture in mind and rely on researchers for updates and news relevant to certain geographical areas and aspects of the campaign. That research is your job, too.

And now that you're focusing on areas that are right for you, the research is interesting to you. Fun, even. What to do?

> Read widely and deeply. This is a big part of your job now. Devote as much time as you can to learning everything about potential job functions and employers that match your priorities and values and may need your talents.

> Research particular businesses or nonprofits that have struck a chord for you. The Web will offer a wealth of information, as will the journals and papers relevant to the field. Take it a step further and do one or both of the following:

  • Investigate volunteer possibilities.

  • Use Vicki Willock's technique (described in chapter 2): make a list of all the professions or jobs that appeal to you and talk with people in each of those fields.

> Read a wide spectrum if you haven't yet discovered what particular industry or field is the best fit. There are association newsletters, journals, white papers, and magazines for every area, profit and nonprofit. Most are available online or at your local library.

  • Read the ones that are particularly relevant to industries and types of organizations you identified after doing the inner Action Items and in your role as campaign manager. By now, you probably have a good sense of what you want for location, type of organization, priorities, culture, and more.

  • Think about what draws you if you're drawn to other publications that don't fit the categories you've chosen. Maybe there's another field to consider.

> Look for information that points out which companies and areas are expanding or hiring. Who is coming out with something new? What particularly sparks your interest? Along the way, you'll find a wealth of information about who works there, what positions they hold, and more. You want to know all you can about industries and companies you may be querying.

- Make a list of all of the organizations or companies that appeal to you based on your priorities, values, strengths, and skills.
- Make a deep list of prospective employers or clients. The bigger the list, the more possibilities. Many successful searchers develop a list of thirty organizations or more.
- Begin to research what job categories are available in the organizations that may be a fit for you. What are the titles of the jobs?
- Develop personalized search engines to keep you apprised of any news relating to these particular companies and any individuals you've identified. It's easy. See www.google.com/cse.

BECOME YOUR OWN CAMPAIGN MANAGER—PART II

As the manager of your own campaign for your right work, there's another role for you. It's what headhunters have done for years. The foundation of every headhunter's success is never-ending networking. Those who don't network constantly, who don't find every opportunity to meet new people, simply don't make it as headhunters. The constant alertness and constant talk has to be fun, has to be energizing. A headhunter has to be comfortable striking up conversations anywhere: in line at the airport, the grocery, elevators, escalators, you name it. Beyond that natural proclivity for networking, what headhunter secrets can you adapt for yourself?

- ➢ The quality of the match of a person's cultural affinity, priorities, and values with the organization itself comes first.
- ➢ When looking for a job, it's better to look for a close fit with the right company than specifically just for the right job. Great jobs grow organically: when employees are well matched to the company, they contribute at a high level and grow both their jobs and their paychecks.
- ➢ It's more productive—and ultimately better—to search for the "right" company first, the "right" job second, and the "right" salary third. More often than not, when the person is really right for the company, the right job will evolve and the right salary will come along with it.

Individuals in search of right work can do a lot for themselves, even without hiring specialized help.

- ➢ Stay proactive, innovative, creative, and positive as much as possible— every single day. (Your mental fitness practice is key here.)
- ➢ Stay open to all options even if they seem to be in the wrong place or wrong industry. (John Racanelli had never contemplated living in Baltimore and now he and his wife Susan love it.)
- ➢ Listen to your inner voice. Strengthen your intuition throughout the process.
- ➢ Don't wait to see job listings before you approach companies for work. Every company has openings before it lists them.
- ➢ Before you respond to an ad in the paper or online or approach a company on your own, reach out to your network to see if anyone knows someone at the company. Ask for an introduction.
- ➢ Headhunters know the success of a search is all about the network. They have the advantage of a network that is deep and wide. You can too, as the next section explains in detail.

UNDERSTANDING NETWORKING—PART II

Back in the outer Action Items, you began work on learning about today's networking possibilities and gathering contact information on the initial group of people who will comprise your network. Now that you've completed the first stages of the self reflection (in the inner Action Items) and defined your values and priorities (earlier in this set of Action Items) it's time to bring your network front and center, to build it, expand it, and actively ask people for help in opening doors and introducing you to their contacts. If the idea of asking for help gives you pause, you may be amazed at how interested people in your network are and how willing they are to help you in support of your quest for right work.

- ➢ Established network: Reach out to each person in the inner circle of your network with a personal phone call. At this point, you're asking for just ten minutes of their time, on the phone. In this call, you'll want to cover the following:

- Explain that you are searching for right work. Tell them the parameters of right work for you. Describe, in one or two sentences, what is important to you relative to work and what you're asking of them. Example:

    I'd like to work for a company in the San Francisco Bay Area that is associated with the software sector. I have strong experience and talent in project management and I speak Mandarin. May I send you my résumé in case you hear of anything?

    This is a short, straightforward explanation paired with a simple request. If the answer is yes, you'll be providing the following:

    - A personalized email that is easy to forward and that includes a bulleted list of your target companies, your objective, and related experience and skills.
    - Your résumé as a Word document. Include lots of white space in your résumé. Less is more.

- Ask each person whether you can include them in a periodic email query when you hear of openings in specific companies since they or someone in their network may well have contacts there. Let them know you'll have an easy way for them to opt out of your mailings if they choose. Be sure to also ask whether
    - they have any recommendations of related areas and companies to research or pursue, and
    - they would be willing to send your résumé directly to people in their networks.

    Before closing the conversation, express how grateful you are to them for their time and help.

- Send out periodic communication to your established network as you complete these conversations and develop your email list (only of those you have spoken with and received approval):
    - Update your list of your target companies, people or organizations (those companies you've researched and are interested in).

- Ask whether anyone can introduce you once you hear of openings and needs in a specific company.
- Be considerate of people's privacy and time. Send your emails as BCCs, with people's names and addresses hidden. Provide a link in your email for people to opt out.
- Thank your contacts for their time and help.

➤ Expanding your network. Once you've determined your areas of interest and the parameters of your right work, use your creativity and contact those people in your existing network who can help put you in touch with the right people.

- In person.
  - Life is one networking opportunity after another. You don't need a special networking event to network. Your next best contact could be someone you meet in line at the grocery store, in an elevator, in class, while volunteering, on the ferry. Get started, and you'll find you can grow your network anywhere and everywhere.
  - Everyone you meet is a potential help to you and you to them. People are interdependent in every imaginable way and we are wired to love to help each other. Don't be shy about asking for help or offering it.
  - As you make new contacts, watch for those who may have relevant contacts for your interests. Reach out to them with a phone call as you did your established network to provide background on your journey and to see if you may include them in your email network.
- Via social media. If you're practicing the Action Items in order, you're already thinking about LinkedIn, Facebook, and other forms of social media. (If not, go back to the outer Action Items, "Prepare to Be Prepared.") Now's the time to plug into social media to exponentially increase the size of your network. In my opinion, for business and professional connections, LinkedIn comes first. It is a remarkable resource.

- ○ LinkedIn. As part of one of my job hunting workshops, "Looking for Jobs in All the Wrong Places,"™ Todd Colbeck joined us and explained to participants that there are four goals for professional networking: getting the word out, gathering information, talking to insiders, and getting in touch with the decision maker who has the authority to hire you. Through LinkedIn, you can readily meet these goals and reach ever-expanding groups of people. "Follow" companies in which you have an interest. Join groups that are relevant to your interests and target companies.

- ○ Facebook. Use social networking sites such as Facebook to expand your network as much as possible. Through your friends and your friends' friends, you're sure to find people who can help you in your search for your right work.

- ○ Other. Social media opportunities are constantly changing. Stay in a learning mode all the time! Individual commitment to lifelong learning is a critical trait for success.

- ➢ Leveraging your growing network. Having spent time developing a strong network, what now?

  - By now you are sending periodic email blasts to your network and you're contacting individuals in your network who have direct ties to your fields of interest.

    - ○ When you have a more clear focus on the direction and the specific parameters of your right work or potential clients for your own business, email your network again to bring them up to date.

    - ○ Understand that you should aim for depth and breadth in your network. The actual size depends on your stage in life and your field.

  - Remind yourself that since networking is a continuing process, you'll want to make developing your network a daily habit, as natural to you as breathing.

  - Even after you're in your current right work, you'll want to continue maintaining and expanding your network. You will find many ways in which you can keep learning through your network and help others in the process.

Once you've discovered the specific parameters of your right work and created or found work that is aligned with your values and priorities and in which you can contribute your strongest skills, talents, and abilities, you may be surprised at how productive and happy you become. When you're doing work that is right, most days are a joy and your energy is constantly renewed. As Robert Mondavi said, "Find work you love and you'll never have to work a day in your life." I can attest to that, for even after decades of finding the right match for my clients and helping candidates identify their right work, I still feel great joy when I have made a match that pairs the candidate with the right work and the company with the right employee. And I get paid for it!

Even when you know you are in current right work, be sure to build in time for periodic evaluation, time to revisit your dreams, intentions, and priorities. Whether it's once a year (perhaps your birthday or the anniversary of discovering your right work) or more often (some people make time for evaluations every spring and fall), be sure to put time for self-evaluation on your calendar and in your mindset. The practice of revisiting priorities periodically helps you ensure that you are aligned with what now matters most in your work life.

Your values generally stay the same, but it's important to make sure they too are still aligned with your company or your work. And when you find a shift going on, you can tap into your inner wisdom. Sometimes all it takes to keep on track with discovering right work is a reassessment of priorities; sometimes the changes are more significant. Bear in mind that your right work is connected closely with your priorities relative to what is happening now in your life. Life is nothing but change and right work changes right along with it. Now that you know how to practice self reflection and know the five steps to right work, each adjustment becomes easier, whatever the time or the purpose.

Remember: you now have the knowledge, tools, and project plan to discover your right work. With that knowledge, commitment, and awareness, you have the security of knowing that you will always be able to create or find your right work—and, guaranteed, be able to create a life you love!

ACKNOWLEDGMENTS

My heartfelt gratitude goes out to my supportive and wide village. I deeply appreciate each and every one of my family, friends, clients, candidates, and acquaintances who steadfastly supported my dream to write this book. Thank you to all those who were my readers and partners on the path.

I thank Sharon Gadberry, my friend and partner in producing the "Home Sweet Office" television shows that were inspired by so many people who had successfully created work and lives they loved.

I've interviewed hundreds of people over the years, each of whom helped me better understand the critical importance of finding right work. I am grateful for each of you, and for the good fortune to have had you in my life. Given how many wonderful stories people shared, it wasn't possible to fit them all into one volume. These stories will be highlighted on the website. A special appreciation for the honor of multiple interviews with the late Robert Mondavi and with the late Warren Hellman.

I have the deepest appreciation for my large extended family and their tireless support of my life. Thank you to Edith Walton Herrick, my Grandma Edie, who passed on the unshakable strength of her Quaker wisdom and guidance and to her husband Myron Collins Herrick, my Baba, who was an entrepreneur, community and business leader as well as a poster child for discovering and succeeding in his right work; to Helene Dieterich Woske, my German Oma, who consistently embodied astoundingly unconditional love and support and to her husband, Max Woske, my Opa, who inspired us as he lived with dignity and tenacity through hardship and challenge. A passionate thank you to my gifted and remarkable father, Harry Woske, an extraordinary parent, healer, teacher, and physician who has exemplified the values of devotion to family and community and service to patients and students; to my late mother, Marcia Herrick Woske, who died much too young; and to Patricia McKiernan, my father's wife and my surrogate mother. Thank you to my sisters Shirley Woske, Lisa Woske (who took talented care with final edits), and Betsy Bragg, and to my "big" brother Tom Woske, all of whom have been devoted, supportive, and fun comrades in life. Heartfelt thanks to my beautiful, talented, and precious daughter Abby Miller Tollefson who is truly the gift that keeps on giving with her tireless support, love, and coaching of me and to her wonderful husband Paul Tollefson for his care of all of us. Thanks and big hugs to my three extraordinary granddaughters, Sophie, Ella, and Cate Tollefson, and to my lovely and talented niece and second daughter, Marcia, who inspires all of us with her creativity and dedication to film.

Thank you to my family of friends, my Issaquah Dock community in Sausalito, and all those who have cheered the project on for so many years. Huge hugs to Jerry Jampolsky and his partner and wife Diane Cirincione, my close friends and neighbors who kept encouraging me, especially when the book seemed too hard to finish. A loving thank you to my partner, Bryant Welch, who has provided unconditional support.

To my patient and nurturing executive assistant and friend, Beth Parker; my Web developer and dear friend, Robin Milam; and Geri Lafferty, who moved Web and marketing projects forward with tenacious vigor: thanks for all of the administrative, technical, and detailed support to the finish. This book wouldn't exist without you and without the efforts of cover designers Susan and Chloe Pate, and interior designer Helen Glenn Court. Thank you all.

A very special thanks to Jan Hunter, my coach, editor, and gentle writing guru. Without your focus and editorial wisdom, I could not have written this book.

My most grateful appreciation, beyond words, to my spiritual teacher Lama Orgyen Chowang Rinpoche. It was through the Buddhist teachings that I began to see vividly how we have the ability to change our experience of life by observing and managing our own minds. Thank you to Giovanna and Rick Brennan who give selflessly in support of the continuation of the Teachings.

ABOUT THE AUTHOR

Leni Miller knows right work. She knows its value to individuals, organizations, and the world at large. Through her right work—work that aligns with her deepest values, priorities, talents and skills—she has helped people find their own right work. Every day, she is thrilled to have a role in helping people take steps—sometimes incremental, sometimes enormous leaps—to their own right work. Guiding people on their way to success and happiness in their work and lives is clearly Leni's passion and her right work.

In four decades as a job placement and search professional, as co-director of the television production "Home Sweet Office," and in her research for this book, Leni has interviewed multiple generations of people in all types of work. Among the common threads and themes, she found that people who were successful and happy had practiced self-reflection and developed the willingness to move confidently in the direction of their dreams, even when they didn't know exactly where their journey would lead them. She also found that without exception, people far on the positive side of the work satisfaction scale, people who are enormously successful and fulfilled in their work have an unending source of energy and happiness.

So it is with Leni. For her, it is an absolute joy to see people's transformation once they are in jobs they love, jobs that energize them and make thorough use of their talents.

Now, with the guidance Leni provides in *Finding Right Work: Five Steps to a Life You Love* readers will be able to discover their own right work, reap the rewards of being in right work, and transform their work and their lives.

An innovative entrepreneur in the business of employment and search, Leni worked for a large staffing agency before founding three separate job placement, consulting, and search companies. An honors graduate of Columbia University, Leni is currently the president of EASearch, LLC, a national firm specializing in recruiting and consulting in the area of senior-level executive support. She has interviewed hundreds of clients in need of high-level executive support and thousands of candidates in search of their right work. Whether it's a tiny startup organization, a Fortune 100 company, or anything in between, Leni understands what support is needed for increased success. She also has a deep understanding of what people need to perform at their best, to thrive in their work and in their lives. Newly minted graduates just dipping a toe in the real world, people who had been dragging themselves to jobs they hated for several years, and seasoned professionals in search of work to reignite their passion have all benefited from Leni's guidance.

Beyond her business and this book, Leni's commitment to helping others is also apparent in her many professional and volunteer roles and affiliations, both past and present, including as a director for Junior Achievement, National Association of Women Business Owners, World Business Academy, and the Center for Attitudinal Healing. In addition, Leni was among the first five women in the world invited to join Rotary in the second oldest Rotary club in the world, the San Francisco Rotary Club.

Leni has learned to celebrate life as it unfolds, being grateful for every moment and challenge. She lives on the Dragon Boat, a well-known floating home in Richardson Bay, in Sausalito, California. She is a kayaker and loves living on the water and within the unique and close community of floating home residents. An avid hiker who loves to travel, Leni has trekked in Bhutan and pushed cattle in Montana. Her daughter Abby Tollefson has definitely found her right work in executive coaching. Leni is confident that each of her three young grandchildren will also find their right work and join the chorus of people who can say, "I just love what I do. I can't believe I get paid for this!"

Made in the USA
San Bernardino, CA
25 April 2014